The Collected Writings of Walt Whitman

# WALT WHITMAN

# Daybooks and Notebooks

## VOLUME III: DIARY IN CANADA, NOTEBOOKS, INDEX

*Edited by* William White

 NEW YORK UNIVERSITY PRESS 1978

# The Collected Writings of Walt Whitman

GRATEFUL ACKNOWLEDGMENT IS MADE TO

## Mr. Charles E. Feinberg,

WHOSE ASSISTANCE MADE POSSIBLE THE ILLUSTRATIONS
IN THIS VOLUME AND WHO ALSO MADE
AVAILABLE TO THE PUBLISHER THE RESOURCES OF
THE FEINBERG COLLECTION.

# CONTENTS

## Volume I

## Volume II

## Volume III

The Collected Writings of Walt Whitman

## Diary in Canada[3389]

June 18 [1880][3390] — Calm and glorious roll the hours here – the whole twenty four. A perfect day, ~~still and~~ (the third in succession) cloudless, the sun clear, a faint, fresh, just palpable air setting in from the Southwest, tem-

3389. The only published version of this material is entitled *Walt Whitman's Diary in Canada, With Extracts from Other of His Diaries and Literary Note-Books,* edited by William Sloane Kennedy (Boston: Small, Maynard & Company, 1904, vi, 73 pp.), issued in a limited edition of 500 copies; as far as I know, it has not been reprinted. The *Diary* portion occupies pp. 1–45; material from other journals, pp. 49–73. It contains a frontispiece of Walt Whitman in London, Ontario, 22 September 1880. The Editor's Preface, pp. v–vi, reads:

The transcribing of these out-door notes from the worn and time-stained fragments of paper (backs of letters, home-made note-books, etc.), on which they were originally written, have been so fascinating a task for me that I feel confident the subject-matter will interest other lovers of Whitman. I don't know that they need any other forword than just the telling how they came into my hands for publication.

In the autumn of 1900 I wrote to my old friend, the late Dr. Richard Maurice Bucke (the senior member of Walt Whitman's literary executors), suggesting that he join me in bringing out a "Readers' Handbook to Leaves of Grass," in the preparation of which I had been engaged for a number of years, by contributing any material he might have that was available. He responded with enthusiasm to this proposal for coöperative work. But, alas! a year later he had passed into eternity.* [Footnote: *He fell on the icy floor of a veranda of his residence, struck on the back of his head, and never regained consciousness. Few knew that this gay-hearted optimist, with his magnificent physique, had to fight his way through life (after twenty) without the aid of feet, other than artificial. His feet were amputated after being frozen in a (finally successful) attempt to cross the Sierra Nevada Mountains in the winter of 1856, in company with one of the two original discoverers of silver in Nevada. I have the romantic printed account of that daring feat.] By his son, Dr. Edward Pardee Bucke, however, I was generously furnished with such manuscripts of Walt Whitman as seem to have been intended for our purpose, and from them the following diary and other notes were selected. The publication of the Readers' Handbook is held over for the present.

In his "Specimen Days," Whitman devotes only a couple of pages to the St. Lawrence and Saguenay trip, — a condensed abstract of his journal.

The portrait used as a frontispiece to this book is reproduced from a photograph by Edy Brothers of London, Ontario, made during the visit to Dr. Bucke recorded in his diary. It has never before been published. All the notes in the volume are by the editor.

W. S. K.

BELMONT, MASS.,
November, 1904.

perature pretty warm at midday, but moderate enough mornings and evenings. Everything growing well, — especially the perennials, — never have I
seen grass and ~~verdure and~~ trees and bushery to greater advantage. ~~in color.~~
All the accompaniments joyous. Cat-birds, thrushes, robins, &c. singing.
~~joyously.~~ The profuse blossoms of the ~~orange-red~~ tiger lily, (is it the tiger-
lily?)[3391] mottling the lawns and gardens everywhere with their glowing
orange red. Roses everywhere too[3392]

[Blank]     [2]

[3]

June & July    Canada '80

Such a procession of long-drawn-out, delicious ~~evenings~~ half-lights, ~~closing,~~
nearly every ~~day~~ evening, continuing on till 'most 9 o'clock, all through the
last ~~half~~ two weeks of June and the first two of July! It was worth coming
to Canada to get these ~~sooth~~ long-stretch'd ~~evenings~~ sunsets, in their ~~linger-
ing~~ temper'd shade and lingering, lingering twilights, if nothing more.

[4]

Canada

[No date.] — It is only here in large portions of Canada that wondrous
second wind ~~of summer~~, the Indian Summer) attains its amplitude and a
heavenly perfection, — the temperature, the sunny haze, the mellow, rich,
delicate, almost flavored ~~of the~~ air:
   "Enough to live — enough to merely be."
See page 774 Vol 4 Enc: Brit: for a ¶ on timber-rafts on the St L

[5]

June 19, '80 – Canada

On the train from London to Sarnia – 60 miles.[3393]

3390.  W. S. K.'s footnote: "Whitman left Camden on June 3 ('on a first-class sleeper')
for Canada. Passed Niagara June 4, and has described his impressions of it as seen on this
particular occasion (*Specimen Days,* p. 160, 1st ed.) On June 4 he writes, 'I am domiciled at
the hospitable house of my friends Dr. and Mrs. Bucke, in the ample and charming garden
and lawns of the asylum.'"
3391.  W. S. K.'s footnote: "Probably the Turk's Head lily (*Lilium superbum*)."
3392.  At this point in the published version is a paragraph not in the extant MS: "A
stately show of stars last night: the Scorpion erecting his head of five stars, with glittering
Antares in the neck, soon stretched his whole length in the south; Arcturus hung overhead;
Vega a little to the east; Aquila lower down; the constellation of the Sickle well toward
setting; and the half-moon, pensive and silvery, in the southwest."
3393.  W. S. K.'s footnote: "Sarnia (the former home for ten years of the late Dr. R. M.
Bucke, when a practising physician) is a town of about 7000 inhabitants lying on the St. Clair
River (Canadian side) near Lake Huron, about 55 miles northeast of Detroit."

A fine country, many good farms, plenty of open land, the finest strips of woods, clean of underbrush — some beautiful ~~clumps~~ clusters of great trees — plenty of fields with the stumps standing, some bustling towns

Strath~~ford~~roy
~~Ruskrow~~
Watford

Point Edward, this side
Fort Gratiot the Michigan
Grand Trunk.

[6]

Canada '80
<u>Sunset on the St Clair</u>
July ~~20~~ 19 – Sunset

I am writing this on Front Street close by the river, the St Clair, on a bank. The ~~sun~~ setting sun, ~~is~~ a great blood red ball ~~of fir~~ is just descending on the Michigan shore, ~~leaving~~ throwing a bright crimson track ~~in the~~ across the water to where I stand ~~on the bank.~~ The river is full of row-boats

[7]

and shells, with their ~~tight~~ crews of young fellows, or single ones, out practising, a handsome, inspiriting Sight. Up north I see ~~? what is the name the~~ at Point Edward, on Canada side, the tall Elevator in Shadow, with tall-square turret like some old castle.

As I write a long shell, with its ~~light-dressed~~ crew of four ~~with nothing~~ stript to their rowing shirts, sweeps swiftly past ~~me,~~ their oars rattling in their rowlocks.

[8]

Opposite, a little south, on the Michigan shore, ~~is~~ stretches Port Huron. It is a still, moist, voluptuous evening, the twilight deepening apace. In the vapors fly bats, and myriads of big insects. A solitary robin is whistling his call, followed by mellow <u>clucks</u>, ~~no~~ in ~~a~~ some trees near. The panting of the locomotive, and measured roll of cars, comes from ~~Michigan~~ over shore, and occasionally an abrupt ~~whis~~ snort ~~from the~~ or screech, diffused in space. With all these utilitarian episodes

[9]

it is a lovely, soft, soothing, voluptuous scene, ~~and~~ — a wondrous half-hour for sunset and ~~then~~ then the long rose-tinged half-light ~~stretch gray~~ with a touch of gray, we sometimes have stretched out ~~Ie Ju~~ in June, ~~so long after the sunset~~ at day-close – How musically the cries and voices floating in from the river

~~I~~ Mostly while I have been here I have noticed ~~over a a score of~~ those handsome shells and ~~row~~ oar-boats, ~~many~~ some of them rowing ~~magn briskly~~ [?] – superbly ~~some now and then a single rower~~

[10]

— ~~the At nin~~ At ~~half past eight~~ nearly nine, it is still quite light, ~~th though~~ tempered with blue film, but the boats, the river, and the Michigan shores ~~all~~ quite palpable. ~~A great The western~~ The rose-color ~~has~~ still falls ~~not~~ upon every thing. A big river steamer is crawling ~~up~~ athwart the stream, hoarsely hissing. ~~O~~ The ~~t~~ moon in its third quarter is just up behind me. From over in Port Huron come the just-heard sounds of a brass band, practising. Many objects, half-burnt hulls, ~~some~~ partially sunk wrecks, slanting

[11]

or upright poles, throw their black shadows in strong relief on the clear glistering water

[12]

### A far-off reminiscence

[London Canada] June 20 [1880] — I see to-day in a New York paper ~~to-day~~ an account of the tearing down of ~~the the an~~ old St Ann's church, Sands and Washington streets, Brooklyn, to make ~~on~~ room for ~~a landing and roadway for~~ the East River Bridge landing and roadway. Away ~~here~~ from here, nearly 1000 miles ~~off~~ distant, it roused the queerest ~~old~~ reminiscences, which I feel to put down and send. ~~It~~ St Ann's was ~~quite a stately building, and~~ twined with many

[13]

memories of youth to me. I think the church was built about 1824, the time when I, ~~at that time~~ (a little ~~one~~ child of 6 years) ~~first went~~ was first taken to live in Brooklyn, and I remember it so well then and for long years afterwards. ~~Its~~ It was a stately building, with its broad grounds and ~~trees~~ grass, and the aristocratic congregation, and the good ~~Mr~~ clergyman, Mr McIlvaine, (afterwards Bishop of Ohio)[3394] and the ~~building~~ long ~~building~~ edifice for

3394. W. S. K.'s footnote: "Perhaps best known and the most popular preacher in Ohio a quarter-century ago. The son of Whitman's friend, John Burroughs, in 1902 married a granddaughter of this Bishop McIlvaine."

a Sunday School, (I had a se pupil's desk there,) and the fine gardens and many big willow and elm trees in the neighborhood. From it St Ann's started, over 50 years ago, the a strange and solemn military funeral, that of the officers and sailors

[14]

killed by the explosion of the U. S. steamer Fulton at the Brooklyn Navy Yard. I remember well the impressive services and the dead march of the band, (moving me even then to tears) and the led horses, and officers trappings, in the procession, and the black-draped flags, and the old sailors in the funeral procession, and the salutes over the grave, in the old ancient cemetery, in Fulton street, just below Tillary, (now all built over by solid blocks of hus houses, and busy stores.)[3395] I was at school, and at the time of the explosion, and remember heard the strange jar rumble of the powerful explosion, which r jarred half the city. Nor was St Ann's (Episcopal) the only

[15]

church, with bequeathing old Brooklyn reminiscences. Just opposite, within stone's throw, on Sands street, with a high range of steps, was stood the main Methodist temple church, always with drawing full congregations, always active, singing, and praying in earnest, and the scene in those days of the powerful revivals of those days, (often continued for a week, night and day, without intermission.) This latter was the favorite scene of the labors of John N Maffit, the famous preacher of his denomination. (It was a famous church for pretty girls.) The ¶ The history of those two churches would be the a history of the Brooklyn, for for and of a main part of its families, of for the earlier half of its the nineteenth century

[16]

[from Sarnia]
    A moonlight excursion up Lake Huron.

June 21. — A moonlight excursion up Lake Huron. We were to go start at 8 p. m., but after waiting forty minutes later for a bra music-band, which, to my secret satisfaction, didn't come, and we, and the Hiawatha went off without it.

Point Edward on the Canada Side and Fort Gratiot on the Michigan, are form the crossing line for the Grand Trunk RR, and looking well-alive with lights, and the sight of shadowy-moving cars, were quickly passed between

3395. W. S. K.'s footnote: "The Whitmans then lived in Tillary Street, where the father had built them a house."

by our steamer, after pressing through ~~the~~ currents of rapids for a mile along here, very dashy and inspiriting — and we were soon out on the

[17]

wide ~~stretch~~ sea-room of the Lake. The far and faint-dim shores, the cool night-breeze, the plashing of the waters, and, most of all, the ~~hour-high~~ well-up moon, full and round and refulgent, were the features of ~~our~~ this pleasant water-ride, ~~on the Hiawatha~~ which lasted till midnight.

[18]

During the day I had seen the magnificent steamboat City of Cleaveland come ~~down~~ from above, and after making a short stop at Port Huron opposite, sped on her swift and stately way down the St Clair; she ~~had~~ plies between Cleaveland and Duluth, and was on her return from the latter place — makes the voyage in three ? days. At a Sarnia wharf I saw the Asia ~~here~~, a large steamboat for ~~the~~ Lake Superior trade and ~~tr~~ passengers; understood there ~~are~~ were three other boats on the line. Between Sarnia and Port Huron some nice small-sized boats are constantly plying. I went aboard the "Dormer" and made an agreeable hour's jaunt to and fro, one afternoon.

[19]

A Sarnia Public School

Stopt impromptu at the school in George ? where I saw crowds of boys out at recess, and went in without ceremony among them, and so inside, for twenty minutes, to the school, at ~~at~~ its studies, music, grammar, &c. Never saw a healthier, hansomer, more intelligent or decorous collection of boys and girls, some 500 altogether. This twenty minutes' sight, and what it inferred, is among my best impressions and recollections of Sarnia.

[20]

W^m Wawanosh

over 400 Indians
                                    Sarnia   June  '80.
Ah me je wah noong
i. e. Rapids
Chief Summer [ ? ]    at present

4 miles by 3   along the St Clair

pop of Sarnia   ~~bet~~ 5000

the whole Dominion    four & a half millions

Ontario nearly two millions[3396]

[21]

Went down to an Indian settlement at Ah-me-je-wah-noon, (the Rapids) to visit the Indians, the Chippewas. ~~There w~~ Not much to see, of novelty — in fact nothing at all of aboriginal life or personality; but I had a fine drive with the gentleman that took me, Dr McLane, the physician appointed by the government for the tribe.

[22]

There is a long stretch, ~~of land,~~ three or four miles, fronting the ~~lake,~~ St Clair, south of Sarnia, running back easterly nearly the same distance, good lands for farming, and ~~a~~ rare sites for building — and this is the "reservation" set apart for these Chips. There are said to be 400 of them, but I ~~did~~ could not see evidences of one quarter that number. There are three or four neat third-class wooden dwellings, a church and council–house

[23]

but the less said about the rest of the edifices the better. "Every prospect pleases," as far as land, shore and water are concerned, however. The Dominion government keeps entire faith with ~~them,~~ these people, (and all its Indians, I hear,) preserves these reservations for them to live on, ~~and~~ pays them regular annuities, and whenever any of their land is sold, ~~put~~ puts the proceeds strictly in their funds. Here they farm languidly, (I saw some good wheat) ~~and~~ fish &c. but the young men generally go off to ~~for~~ hire as laborers and

[24]

deck-hands on the water. I saw and ~~talked~~ conversed with Wa-wa-nosh the interpreter, son of a former chief. He talks and writes as well as I do. In a nice cottage near by lived his mother, who dont speak any thing but Chippewa. There are no very old people. I saw one man of 30, in the last stages of consumption. This beautiful and ample tract, in its present undeveloped condition is quite an eyesore to the Sarnians.

[25]

Tennyson's "De Profundis."
June 24 –

3396.   The material on this page of the MS is omitted in the published version.

To-day I spent half an hour, (in a recluse summer-house embowered,) ~~rea~~ leisurely reading Tennyson's new poem "De Profundis." I should call the piece, ~~a~~ (to coin a term) a specimen of the mystical-recherché — and a mighty ~~superb~~ choice specimen. It has ~~some~~ several ~~deli sparkli~~ exquisite little ~~presentations of~~ verses, not simple like rose-buds, but gem-lines, like garnets or sapphires, cut by ~~an artis~~ a lapidary artist. These, for instance, (some one has had a baby:)

> "O young life,
> Breaking with laughter from the dark!"
>                 "O dear Spirit half-lost
> In thine own shadow and this fleshly sign
> That thou art thou — who wailest being born."

Then from "the Human Cry" attached:

> "We feel we are nothing — for all is Thou and in Thee;
>   We feel we are something — that also has come from Thee."

~~The piece soun~~ ~~It sounds like organ playing,~~

Some cute friends afterward said it was altogether vague, and could not be grasped. Very likely; it sounded to me like organ-playing, <u>capriccio</u>, which also can not be grasped.

[26]

Ontario Canada

<u>The Stars</u>

Night of Saturday    July 3    good night for stars & heavens

perfectly still & cloudless    fresh & cool enough

~~twilights~~ evenings very long, ~~a~~ pleasant twilight till 9 o'clock, all through the last half of June & first half of July

[27]

A long, long twilight after sunset, sometimes lasting till 9 o'clock.[3397] These are my most pleasant hours. The air is pretty cool, but I find it enjoyable, and like to saunter the well–kept ~~tra~~ roads.

The volume of the rivers, lakes, &c. ~~are all full~~ here, is at its fullest[3398]

---

3397. This sentence is omitted in the published version.
3398. This sentence is omitted in the published version.

[28]

<u>Ontario</u>, Canada   July 3 '80

July 3  '80 — Saturday night — Went out ~~to-night~~ about 10 on a solitary ramble in the grounds, slow through the fresh ~~night~~—[ ? ]— air, over the gravel walks and velvety grass, with many pauses, many upward gazings. It was again an exceptional night for the show and sentiment of the stars — very still and clear, not a cloud, and neither warm nor cold. ~~The~~ High overhead, the constellation of the Harp; ~~hung overhead;~~ south of east, the Northern Cross — in the Milky Way the Diadem — and more to the north Cassiopea; ~~and In the Milky Way the Diadem Arcturus~~ bright Arturus and silvery Vega dominating aloft. But the heavens everywhere studded so thickly — ~~great~~ layers ~~on upon~~ on layers of phosphorescence, spangled with those still orbs, emulous, nestling so close, with such light and glow everywhere, flooding the soul

[29]

Sunday evening, July 4 '80

A very enjoyable hour or two, this evening.

They sent for me ~~this evening,~~ to come down in the parlor to hear my friend, M. E. L. a deaf and dumb young woman give some recitations, (of course by pantomime, not a word spoken) She gave first an Indian legend, ~~very pretty,~~ the warriors, the women, the woods, the action of an old Chief, &c., very expressive. ~~Then~~ But best of all, and indeed a wonderful performance, she rendered <u>Christ</u> <u>stilling</u> <u>the tempest</u> (from Luke is it?)

[30]

[London]   Canada   July 6 '80

<u>Haymaking</u>. — July 5, 6, 7. — I go out every day ~~for~~ two or three hours, for the spectacle of ~~in the hay  fields  a~~ a sweet, poetic, practical, ~~stirr~~ busy sight. Never before ~~were there~~ such fine growths of clover and timothy everywhere as the present year; and I never saw such large fields of rich grass, as on this farm. I ride around in a low, easy basket-wagon

[31]

~~with~~ drawn by a sagacious pony; we go ~~every where~~ at random, — over the flat just-mown ~~odorous~~ layers and all around, through lanes and across fields. ~~The great~~ The ~~odor~~ smell of the cut ~~field~~ herbage, ~~The~~ the whirr of the mower, ~~the p~~ the ~~rak~~ trailing swish of the horse-rakes, ~~the wag~~ the forks of the busy pitchers, & the loaders on the wagons — I linger long and long to absorb them all. Soothing, sane, odorous hours! Two weeks of such

[32]

It is a great place for birds, (no gunning here, and no dogs or cats allowed) — I never before saw so many robins, nor such big fellows, nor so tame.[3399] You look out over the lawn any time, and can see from four or five to a score of ~~of~~ them hopping about. I never ~~be~~ before heard ~~the~~ singing wrens (the common house wren, I believe) either — to such advantage ~~There are two specimens at houses I have staid — many times~~ — two of them, these times, on the verandahs of different houses where I ~~was~~ have been staying — such ~~a~~ vigorous, musical, well fibred little notes! (What must the winter wren be, then — they say it is far ahead of this.)

[33]

### Canada – July 8 ’80

~~Haymaking~~ – ~~En~~ I am in the midst of hay-making, and though but a looker-on I enjoy it greatly, untiringly, day after day. Any hour I hear the sound of scythe sharpening ~~a scythe,~~ or the ~~The~~ distant rattle of ~~the~~ horse-mowers, or see the ~~pi~~-loaded ~~hay~~ wagons, high-piled, slowly wending toward the barns, or ~~at~~ toward sun-down groups of ~~sweating~~ tan-faced men, going ~~home~~ from work.

[34]

~~The~~ To-day (July 8) we are indeed ~~in~~ at the height of it here in Ontario[3400] — a week of perfect

[35]

? Glendale

*the ~~long clear continued~~ long-reiterated ~~quaver~~ notes of the robin, ~~firm~~ clear & mellow & ~~continued~~ reedy note — [used elsewhere

W. S. K.]

[No date]. ~~x~~ In the woods, ~~cloudy~~ the days cloudy and moist, but mild & pleasant — the undisturbed rankness of everything — the delicious aroma of the pines in the sweet air — ~~the~~ distant ~~sound~~ shouts from the play-ground of a country school — ~~enough birds~~ in the recesses to the left a bird whistling sharply at intervals — to the ~~left~~ right * (up) – ~~(then back) x2~~

---

3399. W. S. K.'s footnote: "The editor of this diary has the same to record of the robins of southern Wisconsin in the same latitude. They have a larger and fresher look than Eastern robins."

3400. All of the material in the MS from here to ". . . (then back) x2" is omitted in the published version.

[36]

~~the~~ a muffled and musical clang of cow-bells from the grassy wood-edge, not far distant

[37]

July 10 – 14 – Canada, '80[3401]

the ~~blue flower~~ delphinium flower paramount and profuse with its clear blue yellow lilies   profusion of white verbenas, ~~prettily~~ delicately spotting the green lawns   many straw-colored hollyhocks   many ~~beautiful, lots, rose~~ like roses — others pure white  ~~clusters~~ lots of them, beautiful, clusters everywhere on the thick ~~lines of the~~ dense hedge-lines ~~everywhere~~ aromatic white cedars at evening   red Canadian ? honeysuckle     roses have been in great profusion but now flower

[38]

July 10 – 14 – Canada – '80

---

~~on~~ the fences, ~~and~~ verandahs, gables covered with grape-vines and ivies, honeysuckle – a certain clematis (the Jack Manni) bursting all over with ~~its long-lasting~~ deep purple ~~blossoms~~ blossoms, ~~with their~~ each with its four (or five) great ~~blossoms~~ leaves, tough — but delicate as some court lady's dress, but tough and durable, day after day. . . . . — I afterwards saw a ~~wh~~ large ~~white~~ six-leaved ? one of pure satin-like white — as beautiful a flower as I ever beheld.

[39]

Canada – July, 80
        (in blossom now)
Lilium Aurantium a native of Italy [in another hand] 3 ft–35
yellow-red lilies   great profusion   2 ft.
Lilium Aurantium Minor   [in another hand]

—   —   —   —   —

Lilium Buschanium   [in another hand]    1 ft [ ? ]

—   —   —   —   —

---

    little yellow flower
Cosmidium Burridgeanum yellow Coreopsis like flower [in another hand] same as I saw Sept. 79

---

3401. The material in the MS from here to the paragraph headed "Swallow-Gambols" is considerably edited in the published version.

blue, 4 feet high    great profusion
  Delphinium    Blue flower    [in another hand]

---

wild tansy, weed ~~abt~~ from 10 to 15 inches high, white blossom, out in July (middle) in Canada

[40]

July 13 – 14 '80
Canada

The Virginia creeper

---

"Canadian honeysuckle

---

"petunia the little trumpet-shaped petunia with its red and white quarterings

---

at night the aromatic smell of the white cedar

---

oceans of milk white verbenas, and countu [?]
oceans of salmon-colored and scarlet ones

---

—~~pure~~ vast spread of pure sky overhead, of lumped pearly hue, and other vast spread, here in these spacious grounds, of well-kept, close-cropt grassy lawns

[41]

Canada July 18 '80

Swallow-Gambols. — July 18 – ~~For~~ I spent a long time to-day ~~I have been~~ watching ~~the what I name at the head of this parag~~ the swallows — an hour this forenoon, and another hour, afternoon. There is a pleasant secluded close-cropt grassy lawn ~~of~~ a couple of acres or over, flat as a floor, & surrounded by a flowery and bushy hedge, just off the road adjoining the house — a favorite spot of mine. Over this open grassy area, immense numbers of swallows have ~~to-day~~ been sailing, ~~cir~~ darting, circling, and cutting large or small 8's and S's, close to the ground, for hours to-day. It is evidently

[42]

for fun altogether. I never saw anything prettier — this free swallow-dance. They kept it up, too, the greater part of the day.

[2: flyleaf]

'78^{3402}

<u>St. Lawrence</u>
<u>& Saguenay trip</u>
<u>July & Aug: 1880</u>
Quebec notes
To Start  f'm
70 McTavish
M
International R R and Steamship
June
R Chisholm & Co
37 Chaboillez Sq    [?]
20 cts

[2: flyleaf verso]

Isabel Walker / Asylum / Hamilton [in another hand]

[2:1 blank]

[2:2]

### Distances

|  | Miles |  |
|---|---|---|
| Sarnia to London | 60 | |
| London to Toronto | 120 | |
| Toronto to Kingston | 161 | [changed] |
| Kingston to Montreal | 172 | [changed] |
| Montreal to Quebec | 180 | [hence total |
| Quebec to Tadousac | 134 | is wrong] |
| Tadousac to Chicoutimi | 101 | |
|  | 908 | |

3402. The editor of the published version at this point describes the MS: "[Here follows Whitman's journal of his midsummer trip with Dr. R. M. Bucke down the St. Lawrence and up the Saguenay rivers (Montreal, Quebec, Thousand Islands, Cape Eternity, Trinity Rock, etc.). The journal is written on the pages of a thick pocket 'heft' (as the Germans call an extemporized book of stitched leaves), 5 by 8¼ inches in dimensions, and is labelled 'St. Lawrence and Saguenay Trip, July and Aug. 1880.' It is prefixed by a table of distances and a skeleton itinerary (which here follow), has three maps pasted in, covering the entire route, and contains various minor memoranda (names, addresses, etc.) scattered here and there, usually on the verso of the sheet.]"

In the version from the original MS, published here, I am leaving the material as close as possible in type to Whitman's without the "refinements" which William Sloane Kennedy made in his perfectly acceptable reading version. As a posthumous publication, this diary or journal ought to be, it seems to me, just the way Whitman left it — we have no choice, in fairness to him.

from Phila: to London
        about 520 miles

                453

[2:3]

~~leave~~ left London                see back
        July 26 – 8 40 a.m.
            ~~arrive~~ by Great Western R R —
arrived at Toronto – at noon same day (July 26)
left Toronto, noon 27th by Steamboat Algerian
arrived at Kingston early a. m. 28th
Staid at Kingston 6 days
        (Dr Metcalf) Thousand Island Hub House
Left Kingston Aug 3d   at 5 a m
        got to Montreal same evening (Aug 3d)
Staid there 3d & 4th — left 5th p m
– on to Quebec   &
    ——   ~~Quebec Aug 6 a m~~
        ~~leave immediately~~
    ~~(4th by Quebec to~~

[2:4 blank]

[2:5]

Tadousa – ~~get there~~ evening the 6th. ~~same evening of 6th  stay there 1½~~ ~~days Txxx Then & Night (of 6th)~~ & in Steamer <u>Saguenay</u> up the Saguenay same night ~~(voyage up night)~~     reach'd Chicoutimi next morning & Ha-ha bay that night 7th — down the Saguenay again Saturday (7th) to Tadousac (táj-oo-sák) Saw Cape Eternity & Trinity Rock — pass Tadousac & Rivier du Loup 4 p m, 7th (on our return now remember) — reach'd Quebec on Sunday morning 8th at 7½ a m (cloudy wet morning) — Staid over Sunday & Monday – left on the 9th at 5 p m – on "Montreal", arr in M 10th at 8 a m — then straight through in the steamboat Algerian to ~~Hamilton~~ Toronto Aug 12 a m — ~~home on the 14th~~ thence 10.30 a m to Hamilton 12th Aug by R R   back hom to London Aug: 14

[2:6 blank]

[2:7]

        Canada
        <u>July 26 1880</u>

Started this morning at 8 40 from London for Toronto 120 miles by R R —
I am writing this on the cars, very comfortable – We are now (10 – 11 a m)
passing through a beautiful country – it Rained hard last night & showery
this morning – and every thing is looking fresh bright & green. I am enjoying the R R ride, (in a big easy R R chair, in a roomy car)   The am atmosphere is cool, moist, just right, and the sky veiled. We pass through the
thriving towns

[2:8 blank]

[2:9]

Canada – July '80

of Ingersoll, Woodstock, Paris, Harrisburgh, Dundas, & on to Hamilton (80
miles through                counties) a all pleasant, fertile county, sufficiently diversified, frequent signs of cleared land not long cleared, plenty of
black stumps (often the fields fenced with the roots of them) – patches of
beautiful woods, beech, fine elms,        – thrifty ap apple orchards, the grass
hay and wheat mostly harvested, barley begun, oats almost ready, good
farms – plen some good farms – (a little hilly between Dundas & Hamilton
and the same on to Toronto)   Corn looking well, potatoes ditto, but the
great show-charm of my ride is from the unfailing grass and woods.
    Hamilton a bustling city

[2:10 blank]

[2:11]

    As we approach Toronto every thing looks doubly beautiful – especially
the glimpses of the blue Ontario's waters, haz sunlit, yet with a slight haze,
and through which occasionally a distant sail, or two.
    In Toronto at half past 1. I rode up on top of the omnibus with the
driver – the city made the impression on me of a lively dashing place. The
lake gives it its character

[2:12 blank]

[2:13]

Canada

in Toronto, July 27 '80

--------

Front St, wholesale   pretty solid and

Church street
King street, stores, ladies Shopping ("the Broadway")
Sherbourne st.  Jarvis st  &c  long and elegant streets of semi-rural resi-
    dences, many of them very costly & beautiful

————

The horse-chestnut is the prevalent tree – you see it everywhere
The mountain-ash now with its bunches of red berries[5403]
Queen's Park
The Insane Asylum
Mercer's Reformatory for Females

[2:14 blank]

[2:15]

Toronto University, with its Norman architecture, and ample grounds
Knox college
    Mr   Dent
    Mr   Tully the architect

[2:16 blank]

[2:17]

James W. Slocum
      24 Macomb Avenue
          Detroit
           Michigan
Wagner Car Conductor        [5 lines not in Whitman's hand]

————

    July 27  Canada
    I write this in Toronto, aboard the steamboat, the <u>Algerian</u>, 2 o'clock
p m. We are ~~just~~ off presently. The boat ~~with~~ from Lewiston, New York,
has just come in – the usual hurry & with passengers & freight – ~~and~~ as I
write, I hear the pilot's bells, the thud of hawsers unloosened, and ~~and~~ feel
the boat squirming + slowly from her ties, out into ~~the water's~~ freedom.
We are off, off into Toronto bay, (~~and~~ soon the wide expanse & cool breezes
of Lake Ontario)   As we

[2:18 blank]

————

    3403.  The material in the MS from here to the line beginning, "I write this in Toronto,"
is omitted in the published version.

[2:19]

~~get off~~ steam out a mile or so, we get a pretty view of Toronto, ~~as it shows~~
~~it shows from the~~ from the blue foreground of the waters – the whole rising
spread of the city, – groupings of ~~sp~~ roofs, spires trees, ~~banks~~ hills in the
background   ~~At~~ Good bye Toronto, with your ~~fine~~ memories of a very lively
& agreeable ~~day~~ visit[3404]

    ~~Dr.~~ Mr Dent, Dr Clarke & your James Slocum

      Sherbourne & ⎫ long streets
         Jarvis Sts ⎬ fine residences

Front    ⎫
Church    ⎪   business
King &    ⎬   & stores
Yonge   Sts ⎭ King st   the Broadway

[2:20 blank]

[2:21]

A Day & Night on            Canada            A Day on
Lake Ontario                                   Lake Ontario

     On Lake Ontario   July   27  '80
    (Going from   Toronto   to   Kingston)

We start from Toronto about 2 p m. in the Hamilton and Quebec steamboat, (~~pretty~~ middling good-sized and comfortable ~~for~~ carrying shore-freight
and summer passengers.)
(See back for lines)

~~The whole afternoon is~~ Quite a voyage – ~~the~~ the whole length of Lake
Ontario — very enjoyable day – clear, breezy, and cool enough for me to
wrap my blanket around me, as the ~~day lengthens. at times~~ as I pace the
upper deck – For the first 60 or 70 miles we ~~lean~~ keep near the Canadian
shore – of course no land in sight the other side – stop at Port Hope, Coburg,
&c – and then stretch out toward the mid-waters of the lake.

I pace the deck, or sit till pretty late, wrapt in my blanket enjoying all,
the coolness, darkness — and then to my berth awhile.

[2:22 blank]

   3404.  In place of the next few lines in the MS, the printed version reads: "[Entry here
of the name of James W. Slocum, of Detroit, Wagner car conductor, and memorandum 'your
James Slocum.']"

[2:23]
Canada – July 27 '80

- rose soon after 3 to come out on deck and enjoy a magnificent night-show ~~and~~ before dawn. ~~The~~ Overhead, the moon, (at her half and waning ~~and at her~~ half), with lustrous Jupiter, and Saturn, ~~were in~~ made a trio-cluster close together, ~~overhead,~~ in the purest of skies — with the groups of the Pleiades and Hyades ~~fo~~ following ~~them~~ a little off to the east. The lights on the islands and rocks, the splashing waters, the many shadowy shores and passages through them in the crystal atmosphere, the dawn-streaks of faint red and yellow in the east, ~~and yet much else,~~ made a ~~wondrous good wondrous~~ good hour ~~and over~~ for me. We landed on Kingston wharf just at sunrise.

[2:24 blank]

[2:25]

Lake Ontario

Lake O is 234 feet above sea-level. (Huron is over 500 and Superior over 600)

The Chain of Lakes and river St Lawrence drain 400,000 square miles. The rain-fall on this vast area averages annually a depth of 30 inches ~~deep~~ – so that the existence and supply of ~~these~~ these the river, fed by ~~these~~ such inland preceding seas, is a matter of very simple calculation after all

[2:26 blank]

[2:27]
Canada   July 29 '80

July 28 – ~~This afternoon & evening~~ To day Dr M[etcalf] took me in his steam-yacht a ~~lon good~~ long, lively varied voyage, down among the Lakes of the Thousand Islands. ~~Dr M took me in his little steam yacht~~ – we went swiftly on east of Kingston, through cuts, channels, lagoons ?, and out across lakes — numbers of islands always in sight – often, as we steamed by, some almost grazing us — rocks and cedars — occasionally ~~some members of~~ a camping party on the shores, perhaps fishing — ~~some~~ a little sea-swell on the water — On our return, evening ~~came on~~ deepened, ~~with bringing~~ bringing a miracle of sunset

I could have gone on thusly for days over the savage-tame beautiful element. We had some good ~~Italian~~ music (one of Verdi's compositions) from the band of B battery, as we ~~lay off Shore~~ hauled in shore, ~~and~~ anchored, and listened in the twilight (to the slapping rocking gurgle of our boat) Late when we reached home.

[2:28 blank]

[2:29]

July 29 – This forenoon a long ride through the streets of Kingston, and so out into the country, and the Lake shore road.

describe Kingston

Kingston has a population of 15,000   ~~On The shore some~~ The place is a military station (B battery) shows quite a fort, and half a dozen old Martello towers, (like big conical-topt pound-cakes.) It is a pretty town of 15000 inhabitants

[2:30 blank]

[2:31]

the St Lawrence, including all the Lakes &c. from the sea to Duluth is over 2500 miles

───────

Vessels of 800 tons can now go through; soon 1400 tons[3405]

[2:32 blank]

[2:33]

Canada   July 31 '80

Lakes of the Thousand Islands

Saturday Evening July 31 '80 – I am writing this at ~~at~~ & after sundown in the central portion ("American side" as they call it here) of the Lakes of the Thousand Islands, 25 miles east of Kingston. ~~All is Evening~~ The scene is made up of the most beautiful and ample waters, twenty or thirty woody and rocky islands (~~some~~ varying in size, some large, ~~some~~ others small, others middling) the distant shores of the New York side, some ~~white~~ puffing steamboats in the

[2:34 blank]

[2:35]

open waters, and numerous skiffs and row-boats — all showing ~~b~~ as minute specks in the amplitude and primal naturalness

The brooding waters, the cool and delicious air, the ~~long twilight~~ long

───────

3405.   These two sentences are omitted in the published version.

evening with its transparent half-lights ~~over~~ – the glistening and faintly-slapping waves – the circles of swallows, gamboling and piping — [3406]

I am ~~a sailing~~ up & down ~~about~~ here for two or three, the guest of Dr M in his steam yacht   [add p. at end of this diary

[2:36 blank]

[2:37]

### Canada

Aug 1 '80 – Sunday noon – ~~I am still in the~~ Still among the Thousand Islands, (this is about the centre of them, stretching 25 miles to the east, and the same distance west)   The beauty of the spot, all through the day, the sunlit waters, the fanning breeze, the rocky and cedar-bronzed islets. the larger islands with fields and farms, the ~~white-sail'd~~ white-wing'd yachts and shooting row-boats, — and over all the blue sky arching copious – make a sane, calm, eternal picture, to ~~the~~ eyes ~~and~~ senses ~~of~~ and my soul

Land of the purest Air
Land of the Lakes and Woods

[2:38 blank]

[2:39]

### Canada

### Lakes of Thousand Island

Aug 1 – Evening – An unusual show of boats gaily darting over the waters in every direction – not a poor model among them, and many of exquisite beauty, ~~and~~ grace, and speed. It is a precious experience, one of these long midsummer twilights in these waters, and this atmosphere. Land of pure air! Land of unnumbered lakes! Land of the islets & the woods

[2:40]

[Clipping from a newspaper:][3407]

THE THOUSAND ISLANDS OF THE ST. LAW-RENCE. By Franklin B. Hough, Syracuse,

---

3406.  Here the editor of the published version inserts a paragraph from the back of the diary — following Whitman's instructions — preceded by a notation: "[In the back of the Canada diary is the following, evidently a first draft or memorandum for a letter to some one.]" The two sentences, "I am a *sailing* . . ." and "add p. at end . . . ," are omitted in the published version. The inserted paragraph is printed below, in its proper place, p. |2:160|.

3407.  This is not reproduced in the published version.

N. Y. Davis, Barden & Co., Publishers. Received from J. B. Lippincott & Co., Philadelphia. A part of the attraction of this little book is found in the Canadian boat songs which it contains. The early Indian history of the missions and the expeditions, French and English on rivers and lakes, make up this compendium of tradition and topography — to which are added the "impressions" of numerous travellers.

[2:41]

Canada
Lakes of Thousand Islands

Aug 2 – Early morning – a steady south-west wind – the fresh peculiar atmosphere of the hour & place, worth coming a thousand miles to get. ~~The~~ O'er the waters, the gray rocks and dark-green cedars of a score of big and little islands around me, the added splendour of sunrise. As I sit, the sound of slapping water, to me most musical of sounds

One peculiarity as you go about among the islands, or stop at them, is the entire ~~of~~ absence of horses & wagons. Plenty of small boats however, and always very handsome ones. Even the women row, and sail skiffs. Often the men here build their boats themselves

[2:42 blank]

[2:43]

Canada

Aug 2 '80 – Forenoon, a run of ~~four~~ three hours (some thirty miles [ )], through the islands and lakes, in the "Princess Louise" to Kingston. Saw the whole scene, with its sylvan rocky and aquatic loveliness to fine advantage. Such amplitude – room enough here for the summer recreation of all North America

Gananogue

[2:44]

[Small printed card:] 3408

PLACES OF INTEREST
IN AND ABOUT MONTREAL.

3408. This is not reproduced in the published version.

Court House
New Post Office
New City Hall
Bank of Montreal
Bonsecours Market
McGill College
English Cathedral
French Cathedral

Jesuit Church
The Drive around the
[Mountain
Hotel Dieu Hospital
Mount Royal Cemetery
The Drive to Lachine
Grey Nunnery
Victoria Bridge

The Drive to the Mountain Park.

—:o:—

Distance from Montreal to

| Quebec | 180 | Kingston | 172 |
|---|---|---|---|
| White Mountains | 201 | Toronto | 333 |
| Saratoga | 212 | Hamilton | 372 |
| Albany | 261 | Niagara Falls | 400 |
| New York | 406 | Detroit | 547 |
| Boston | 332 | Chicago | 831 |
| Ottawa | 116 | St. Louis | 1126 |

333
172
———
161

[2:45]

Canada   Aug '80

Aug 4 – In Montreal – guest of Dr T S H [3409] ~~Delightful~~ Genial host, delightful quarters, good sleep. ~~Good~~ Explore the city leisurely, but quite thoroughly: St James' Street, with its handsome shops, Victoria Bridge, the ~~big Cathedral~~ great French church, the English Cathedral, the old French Church of Notre-Dame de Bonsecours, the grandest [?] ~~place I ever saw~~; the handsome new peculiarly and lavishly ornamented church of Notre-Dame de Lourdes

the French streets of middle
~~or~~ life with their signs
a city of 150,000 people
very bustling
principal city north of the St Lawrence
the Hotel Dieu hospital [3410]

3409.  W. S. K.'s footnote: "Dr. T. Sterry Hunt, who first brought Whitman's writings to the notice of Dr. Bucke. He is described by Dr. B. in Walt Whitman Fellowship Papers, No. 6, as a Mineralogist to the Geological Survey of Canada."
3410.  These three lines are omitted in the published version.

[2:46 blank]

[2:47]

but the principal character of Montreal to me, was from a drive ? along the street looking down on the river front & the wharves where the Steamships lay, twenty or more of them, some as handsome and large as I ever saw, beautiful models, trim, two, or three, ~~or four~~ hundred feet long, some moving out, one or two coming in – plenty of room, and fine dockage, with heavy masonry banks.

[2:48 blank]

[2:49]

Canada – Aug 5 '80
forenoon

Three hours on Mount Royal, the great hill & Park back of Montreal. Aug 5, ~~forenoon,~~ occupied. Spent the forenoon with on a leisurely most pleasant drive on ~~the~~ and about this hill –~~fine~~ many views ~~fr~~ of the city below, the waters of the St Lawrence – in the clear air – the Adirondacks 50 miles or more distant – the ~~good roads, Zig Zaging around~~ excellent roads, miles of them, ~~forever~~ or up hill. & down the plentiful woods, oak, pine, hickory – the French sign boards <u>Passez a Droite</u> – as we zig-zag around the splendid views, distances, waters, mountains, vistas, some of them quite unsurpassable – the continual surprises of fine trees, in groups, or singly – the grand, rocky, natural escarpments – frequently open spaces, larger or smaller, with patches of golden rod, or white yarrow, or ∅ along the road the red fire-weed or Scotch thistle in bloom – just the great hill itself, with its rocks & trees unmolested by any impertinence of ornamentation

[2:50 blank]

[2:51]

Canada  Aug  '80                    1
<u>Sunrise – the St L   Near Quebec.</u>

<u>Aug 5 & 6 —</u> Have just seen ~~the~~ sunrise, the great round dazzling ball, straight ahead over the broad waters – a rare view – standing on the extreme bow of the boat.

The shores pleasantly thickly dotted with houses – the river here wide, ~~calm,~~ and looking beautiful in the golden morning's sheen. As we advance north-east the earth-banks high and sheer a ~~(earth, no rocks)~~ quite thickly wooded. — ~~Bright, calm, stately sun rise   sea-like waters, spreading here so~~

~~amply~~ – ~~the~~ thin dawn – ~~has~~ mists quickly resolving – ~~the~~ ~~powerful orb mounting the heavens~~ – the youthful strong warm forenoon ~~asserting itself~~ over the ~~noble waters and~~ high green bluffs

[2:52 blank]

[2:53]

Aug 5 – 6     2

~~th wh~~ along the banks as we steam rapidly little white houses seen through the verdure – occasionally a pretensive mansion, a mill, a two tower'd church, ~~glistening with steeples in zinc~~ in burnish'd tin. A ~~very~~ pretty shore, miles of it sitting up high, well-sprinkled with dwellings of habitans ~~and~~ farmers, fishermen, ~~&c~~ French cottagers, ~~&c~~ &c ~~labor~~ – verdant every where (but no big trees) – for 50 miles before coming to Quebec, these little rural ~~villages~~ cluster-towns just back from the bank-bluffs, ~~very pretty~~ so happy and peaceful looking. I saw them ~~well~~ through my glass, everything quite minutely & fully. In one such ~~little~~ town of perhaps two hundred houses, on sloping ground, ~~a little back from the tr blu bluff fringe of dense green~~ the old church with glistening spire stood in the middle ~~with~~ quite a large grave yard around it. ~~and~~ I could see the white head-stones ~~and~~ almost plainly enough to count them.

[2:54 blank]

[2:55]

Canada   Aug 6 '80   4 (3)

~~Nearing~~ Approaching Quebec rocks & rocky banks ~~ever~~ again, the shores lined for many miles with immense rafts of logs, and partially hewn timber, the hills more broken & ~~picturesque~~ abrupt, the other [?] higher shores crowded with ~~little~~ many fine dormer-window'd houses. ~~Shipping~~ Sail ships appear in clusters with their weather-beaten spars & furl'd ~~sails~~ canvas. The river still ample & grand, the banks ~~high~~ bold ~~&,~~ plenty of round turns and promontories, — plenty of ~~g~~ grey rock cropping out. — Rafts, rafts of logs everywhere. The high ~~fort~~ rocky citadel ~~on it pro~~ thrusts itself out — altogether perhaps (at any rate as you approach it on the water, the sun two hours high) ~~the most~~ as picturesque and appearing city ~~yet~~ as there is on earth.

[2:56 blank]

[2:57]

Aug 6                                Canada    Quebec   5   (4)

~~below~~ To the east of Quebec we pass the large ~~ric~~ fertile Island of Orleans – the fields ~~are cut~~ divided in long lateral strips across the island, and appearing to be closely cultivated. ~~In One~~ In one fìeld I notice them getting in the hay, ~~loading and hauling it~~, a woman assisting, loading and hauling it. The view and scene continue ~~irresistably~~ [?] ~~beau~~ broad and beautiful under the forenoon sun – around me an expanse of waters stretch ~~out of sight~~ fore & aft as far as I can see – outlines of ~~high~~ mountains in the ~~far~~ distance north and south – of the ~~most distant~~ farthest ones the bulk and crest lines showing ~~very delicate~~ through ~~the pretty~~ [?] strong but delicate haze like gray lace

[2:58 blank]

[2:59]

Aug 6th night – we are steaming up the Saguenay[3411]        (5)
[add Ha Ha    Bay forward]

[2:60]

[Clipped half page, right half is p. 2:76; page cancelled with diagonal line.]

Ha-ha bay    Aug 7  '80

✝ have had my fill, the last three days of some of the ~~g~~ tallest savagest scenery on earth

I am here nearly 1000 miles north from Phila ~~a hundred miles~~ away up the Saguenay river in the ~~wildest~~ strangest region you ever see – ~~it does my heart good~~ \I am writing this on ~~the forward deck of~~ the steam~~boat~~er where I sleep and eat for a week – have just had a good breakfast, & am feeling ~~pretty~~ well, for me – a beautiful sunny crispy day day – ~~not too~~ just right from the mountains and gray rocks ~~wild savage scenery~~ in sight everywhere – the river ~~beautiful~~, very fine flowing through~~it~~ all, but the water black ~~as~~ ink – a dark brown sometimes like the ~~boat has been~~ – the crowd of the people at Ha-ha bay here as we get ready to·start all sorts ages, on the wharf, àre a good study to me – ~~every body~~ all speak French you know, 4 (four

3411. The material in the MS from here to the paragraph beginning, "Aug 6 and 7 – Ha-ha bay," is either omitted in the published version or heavily edited. Inserted is a paragraph headed "[*Note at end of diary.*]," and beginning, "Walt Whitman is at Ha Ha Bay. He says . . ." (See below for the short paragraph.)

fifths of this Quebec province ¥ of French), where I ~~have been for~~ am now travelling

[Sheet cut off here.]

[2:61]

20

from Quebec to Chicou     235

I am here ~~due n~~ nearly 1000 miles (slightly east of due north) by way of Montreal & Quebec, from my Phil. s e. starting point in the strangest country

Cold – overcoat – had a good night's sleep but up before sunrise

— northern lights every night

As with overcoat on, or wrapt in my blanket ~~are~~ I plant myself on the forward deck

235
180
403
100
___
918

[2:62]

Buffalo, noon, Friday

All right, so far – had a good trip & a good sleeper & bed, & accomoda-tions – best R R track I ever travelled over – had good breakfast at 8 at Hor-nellsville – am now about 430 miles from Phila: I believe – am feeling all right

[2:63]

Canada     Aug '80          16     6

Aug 6 and 7 – Ha-ha bay. Up the black Saguenay river, – a hundred or so miles – ¾ dashes of the grimmest, wildest, savagest scenery on the planet, I guess – a strong, deep ~~river~~ (always hundreds of feet, sometimes thousands) dark-water'd river, very dàrk, with high, rocky hills – green and gray-edged banks in all directions – no flowers, no fruits (plenty of delicious wild blue-berries and raspberries up at Chicoutimi, though) and Ha-ha bay

[2:64]

[Clipped half page, left half missing.]

~~rst~~ hours ~~of~~ on the forward
night – latter, have to
st around me besides
every night. —[3412]

3412.   This is omitted in the published version.

[2:65]

17½

The priests – Saw them on ~~the~~ every boat, and ~~and~~ at every landing; at Tadousac came a large and handsome yacht, manned and evidently owned by them, to bring some departing passengers of their cloth & take ~~off~~ on others. It looked funny to me at first to see ~~this~~ the movements, ropes and tiller handled by these ~~long black gowns~~ swarming black birds; ~~it must be said too~~ but I soon saw that they sailed their craft skilfully & well.

[2:66 blank]

[2:67]

17

: simple, middling industrious, merry, devout Catholic [,] a church everywhere, (priests in their black gowns everywhere, often groups of handsome young fellows) ~~tow~~ life tones low, few luxuries, none of the modern improvements, no hurry, often big families of children, ~~not~~ nobody "progressive," all apparently living and moving entirely among themselves, taking small interest in the outside world of ⟨politics, changes, news, fashions⟩ industrious, yet taking life very leisurely, with much dancing and music.

[2:68 blank]

[2:69]

18

Again I steam over the Sagenay⟨'s ~~bronze-black waters~~
~~I see~~ The bronze-black waters, and the thin streaks lines of white curd, and
the dazzling ~~silvery~~ sun-dash on the stream
~~The~~ The banks of grim-gray mountains and rocks, ~~are keep the banks~~
~~I see~~ The grim and savage scene[3413]

[Fancies at Navesink / The Pilot in the Mist]

―――――――

~~Made a good breakfast of sea-trout, finishing off with wild raspberries~~
hotels here, a few fashionables but they get away soon – it is ~~pretty~~ almost
cold except the middles of ~~some~~ a few ~~of the~~ July & August days

[2:70 blank]

---

3413. W. S. K.'s notation which precedes these lines: "[Here follows what is evidently a thumbnail sketch for the first part of *Fancies at Navesink*.]"

[2:71]

19

trinity & rock

Ete Cape Eternity

———

great, calm eternal rock
    everywhere a matted green
    covering the mountain sides

———

The inhabitants peculiar to our eyes – many marked characters, ways looks, by-plays, costumes, &c. that would make the fortunes of an actors that who could reproduce them

[2:72 blank]

3    [2:73]

more or less aquatic character runs through the people. Then the two influences of French & Englis British contribute a curious by play
Continual Hamlets and villages of white one-story white washed houses

[2:74 blank]

[2:75]

\ ? On the Saguenay /    13

Many Contrasts all the while. At one place, St Paul's bay, this place, backed by these mountains high & bold, nestled down the h hamlet of St Pierre, apparently below the level of the bay, and very secluded & cosy. Then two or three miles further on I saw a larger town high up on a the plateau.
    At St Paul's bay, a stronger cast of scenery, many rugged peaks.

[2:76]

[Clipped half page; right half is the "missing" half of p. 2:60]

[2:77]

14

On the St L Saguenay

    the noticeable items
on land   the long boxes of blue-berries
(We had over a thousand of them brought carried on board wh at Ha-ha

bay ~~the day I came down~~) one day I was on the pier) the groups of ~~fas~~ "boarders," both men and women (retaining all their most refined toggery) – the ~~queer~~ vehicles, some "calashes," many queer old one-horse top-wagons, ~~every one~~ with an air of faded gentility – on the water, the sail craft and steamers we pass, — out in the stream, the rolling and turning up of the white-bellied porpoises, some special island or rock (often very picturesque in color or form) – all the scenes at the piers as we land ~~for~~ to leave or take passengers and freight, especially many of the natives

[2:78 blank]

[2:79]

15

the changing aspect of the light and the marvellous study ~~it is~~ from that alone, every hour of the day, or night ~~either~~ – the indescribable sunsets and sunrises (I often see the latter now) the glorious nights and the stars, Arcturus and Vega and Jupiter and Saturn, and the constellation of the scorpion — [3414] the scenes at breakfast and the other meal-times (and what an appetite one gets) — the delicious fish (I mean from the cook's fire, hot)

( – I had a good opera-glass and made constant use of it, sweeping every shore)

Northern lights every night

[2:80 blank]

[2:81]

6

Canada   Aug   '80

Quebec ~~come from~~ from the river – Aug 8 '80

Imagine (the angles each a mile long) of a high rocky ~~angular~~ hill flush & bold to the river with plateau on top, the front handsomely presented to the South & east (we are ~~coming~~ steaming up the river), on ~~on~~ the principal height still flush with the ~~river~~ stream, a vast stone fort, the most conspicuous object ~~from the river~~ + in view – the magnificent ~~river~~ St Lawrence itself – many hills and ascents, and ~~p~~ tall edifices ~~in~~ shown at their best, and steeples – the handsome town of Point Levi opposite – a long low sea-steamer just ~~starting~~ hauling out

3414.  For some curious reason, Kennedy omitted these words which are between dashes ("the glorious nights. . . .") from the published version.

[2:82 blank]

[2:83]

John Richardson.
A Battery
Citadel
Quebec[3415]

[2:84 blank]

[2:85]

Canada '80    7

Aug 8 – Sunday forenoon – A ~~long~~ leisurely varied drive around the city, stopping a dozen times and more. ~~W~~ I went into the citadel, ~~&~~ ~~walked~~ talked with the soliers – (over 100   here, Battery A., Canadian militia, the regulars having long since departed. A ~~strong~~ fort under the old dispensation, strong and picturesque as Gibraltar.) Then ~~we went~~ to several Catholic churches, and to the Esplanade.

The chime-bells rang out at intervals all the forenoon, joyfully clanging. ~~I found myself~~ ~~listening~~ It seems almost an art here; I never before heard their peculiar sound to such ~~pleas~~ mellifluous advantage and pleasure.

the old name of Quebec   Hochelega   [Hochelega (ho-shel' a-gah) is derived from a word meaning   means beaver grounds. Ed.]

(add here p on Quebec at end of this diary) [not WW's hand]

[2:86 blank]

[2:87]

8

Quebec   Aug 9 '80

Aug 9 – forenoon We have driven out 6 or 7 miles to the ~~Falls of~~ Montmortenci Falls & I am writing this as I sit high up on the steps, the ~~Falls right~~ cascade immediately before me – the great rocky chasm at my right and an immense lumber ~~station~~ depot bordering the river, far, far below, ~~me~~ almost under me, to the left. It makes a pretty and picturesque show, but not a grand one. The ~~water~~ principal fall 30 or 40 feet wide & $\frac{250}{250}$ feet high roaring and white pours down a slant of dark gray rocks, & there are six or seven rivulet falls ~~with~~ flanking it.   **

3415.  Name and address omitted in the published version.

[2:88 blank]

[2:89]

9

*Every house for miles is ~~built~~ set diagonal[ly] with one of its corners to the road – never its gable or front. The road out here from the city is a very ~~fine~~ good one, lined with ~~good~~ moderate-class houses, copious with women & children – the men appear to be away – I wonder what they work at? (up* — there seems little farming here — & I see no factories –

**Since writing the above I have gone down the steps (some 350) to the foot of the Fall, which I recommend every visitor to do — the view is peculiar and fine. The whole scene grows steadily upon one, & I can imagine myself after many visits forming a finally first-class estimate ? [3416] from what I see here of Montmorenci – over a part of the scaly grim ~~bal~~ bald-black ~~b~~ rock, the water falling down ~~in strings and streaks~~ w downward, like strings of snowy-spiritual beautiful tresses   *

[2:90 blank]

[2:91]

10

Through the forenoon I watched ~~these~~ the cascade under the advantages now of ~~a~~ partly cloudy atmosphere, and ~~partly~~ now of the full sunshine.
the tamarck trees,
the great loaves of bread,
     shaped like clumsy
          butterflies

—

Jo Le Clerc
– our driver
     lifting his fingers

—

groups
  onions
  houses all set diagonally
     long strips
       good kitchen cordins [?] [3417]

3416.  W. S. K.'s footnote: "This word in the MS. has a query above it, — a common habit of Whitman, not only in this diary, but elsewhere, when he felt not wholly satisfied but that he might be able later to write a better word. Very frequently, too, in this diary, a second (alternative) word is written above the first, as if in his mind the choice were doubtful."
3417.  The words from "groups" to here are omitted in the published version.

[2:92 blank]

[2:93]

11

hundreds of (to our eyes) funny looking one-horse vehicles, calashes, antique gigs.

—

*long narrow strips of farms [?] – heavy two-seated covered voitures, d always drawn by one horse.[3418]

—

coarse rank tobacco

—

big-roofed one-story houses with projecting eaves

—

potatoes plenty & fine looking.

—

entire absence of barns   barns

[2:94 blank]

[2:95]

12

doors & windows wide open, saw exhibiting [?] many groups through them to us as we passed

———

the ruins of Montcalm's country-seat   the strong old stone walls still standing to the second story – divided [?] many old stone walls, (including those of the old city) still standing

[2:96 blank]

[2:97]

[Insert from below]     Canada '80

   Aug 10, 8 a m – Again in Montreal. As I write this I am seated aft in the delicious river breeze on the steamboat that is to take me back west some ? 380 miles from here to Hamilton. Two hours yet before we start – few passengers, as they come east by the boats, but and then generally take the Railroad back. Montreal is the has the largest show of sail-ships and sea hand-

---

3418.   Inserted by the editor in the published version: "[as in France]."

some ocean steamers of any place on the + river and lake line, and I am right in full sight of them

tr up)

Aug 9 – ⅄ Very pleasant journey on the of 180 miles this afternoon and to-night. An Crowds of Catholic priests on board with their long loose black gowns and the broad brims of their hats turned into a peculiar triangle

[2:98 blank]

[2:99]

Going on the river westward from Montreal, is a pretty slow & tedious, taking you a long time to get through the canals, & many locks, to Lake St Francis, where the steamer emerges to the river again. These rapids along here – the boats can descend, them, but cannot go up them. A great inconvenience to the navigator, but they are very quite exciting with their whirls, & roar & foam, & very picturesque.

---

(Always accenting the last syllable with a loud tremendous bah!)[3419]

[2:100 blank]

[2:101]

– Saw here too are graveyards  In a lovely little shore-nook, under an apple tree, green, grassy, fenced by rails, lapped by the waters, I saw a grave, & white headstone fo & footstone – could almost read the inscription
Aug 10 Evening was wondrously clear, pleasant and calm. I think it it must have been unusual to have the river – the river was as smooth as glass for hours. All the stars shone in it from below as bright as above, — the young moon an and Arcturus and Aquila, and after 10 lustrous Jupiter  Nothing could be more exquisite – than steaming along in this manner I sat away forward on the by the bow & watched the show till after 11.

[2:102 blank]

[2:103]

Aug 12 – 11 a m – As we take the cars at Toronto to go west, we I miss the first thing I notice is the change of temperature – no more the cool fresh air of the lakes, and more than any thing else Sagu the St Lawrence and the Saguenay.

3419.  This sentence omitted in the published version.

[2:104 blank]

[2:105]

Canada    80

'80

Aug 12 – 4½ p m   I am writing this at Hamilton high up on ~~the~~ a hill south of the town – ~~an~~

Aug 13 p m – I write this on a singular strip of beach off Hamilton and To day have been driving about for several hours – ~~the ro~~ some of the roads high up on the crest of the mountain – spent a pleasant hour in the wine-vaults of Mr. Haskins and another at the vineyard & hospitable house of Mr Paine who treated us to some delicious native wine

[2:106 blank]

[2:107]

Canada    80

August 14 – I am writing this on the high balcony of the Asylum at Hamilton (Ontario Canada)[3420] — The city is spread in full view before me. (Is there not an escaped patient? I see a great commotion, Dr. W. and several attendants, men & women, rushing down the cliff) —

a dark, moist, lowering forenoon – balmy air, though – wind South-west

Aug 14 – 5½ p m – Arrived back in London a couple of hours ago, all right. Am writing this in my room Dr B's house

[2:108 blank]

[2:109]

Canada    '80

Aug 14 – ~~Throu~~ Along the way on the journey from Hamilton to London every where through the car windows I saw ~~the~~ locust trees growing ~~&~~ & the broad yellow faces of sunflowers & the sumach bushes with their red cones, and the orchard trees loaded with apples

[end of his trip]        [add here "lecture" items]

– The waters – the Lakes and the indescribable * grandeur &   ?  of the St Lawrence are the beauty of Canada through this vast line of two thousand miles and over. – In ~~these~~ its peculiar advantages, sanities and charms, I doubt whether the globe for democratic purposes has its equal

3420.  W. S. K.'s footnote: "Dr. Bucke was during the year 1876 medical superintendent of this asylum. — *Free Press,* London, Ont., Feb. 2, 1902 (obituary)."

[2:110 blank]

[2:111]
                                        Canada     ⌐ tr.

? for lecture     for conclusion ? [3421]
———

A ~~great beautiful~~ grand, ~~sand~~ sane, temperate land, the amplest & most
beautiful and      stream of water, a river & necklace of vast lakes, pure,
sweet, eligible, supplied by the chemistry of millions of square miles of gush-
ing springs & melted snows
      ~~a~~ No Stream this for ~~a~~ side <u>frontier</u> – stream rather for the great central
current the glorious mid-artery of the great Free ~~solid Nationality~~ <u>Pluribus
Unum</u> of America – the solid Nationality of the present and the future

[2:112 blank]

[2:113]
the home of an improved grand race of men & women, not of ~~one~~ some
select class, only, but of larger, saner, better masses
      – I should say this vast area (from      lat &      ) was fitted to be
their unsurpassed <u>habitat</u>
      I know nothing finer – the European democratic tourist, philanthropist,
geographer, or genuine inquirer ~~r~~ will make a fatal mistake who leaves
these shores without understanding this — I know nothing finer, either

[2:114 blank]

[2:115]
from the point of view of the sociologist, the ~~ts~~ traveller or the artist, than
a month ['s] devotion to even ~~a~~ the surface of Canada, over the line of the
great Lakes & the St Lawrence, the fertile, populous and happy province of
Ontario, the      of Quebec, with another month ~~or~~ to the hardy mara-
time regions of New Brunswick, Nova Scotia and Newfoundland.

[2:116 blank]

———
3421. Preceding this line, the editor has inserted in the published version: "[A little
farther back in his diary Whitman has the following equally enthusiastic paragraphs of gen-
eralizations on Canada. They are labelled thus: '?For lecture — for conclusion?']." This is
followed by the material below, ending, ". . . Nova Scotia and Newfoundland."

[2:117]

St Lawrence[3422]                                            xx

I see, or imagine I see in the fu[ture]   A race of 2,000,000 farm – families, 10,000,000 people, – every farm running down to the water, or at least in sight of it – the best air and drink and sky & scenery of the globe   the sure foundation-nutriment of heroic men & women – The summers     ?     the winters – I have sometimes doubted whether there could be a great race without the hardy influence of winters, in due proportion

[2:118]

[Rough map, drawn by Whitman, of the St Lawrence River, Saguenay River, Hudson River, showing Montreal and Quebec.]

[2:119]

<u>Canada</u>     St Lawrence

– to me its crowning ~~glory~~ land of the rarest ~~and best~~ & healthiest air (an area of three or four hundred thousand square miles)
— land of clear skies and sunshine of course by no means tropical, ~~and~~ neither in any     ?     degree arctic
– In June, July and August, the long evening twilights – in September and October the most perfect days perhaps vouchsafed to any part of the globe

[2:120  blank]

[2:121]

All in Dominion   except the province of Newfoundland
Ontario 121,260 sq: miles
  Quebec 210,020

total Dominion   3,500,000 sqr M
Quebec
Ontario
Nova Scotia
New Brunswick
Prince Edward Island
British Columbia
Manitoba

3422.  This phrase is omitted in the published version, and the editor has inserted a notation: "[In Whitman's Canadian diary, as I received it, I find the following notes on loose sheets.]" This is followed by the material below, edited heavily, and ending with the paragraphs on the Canadian school system.

Hudson Bay & North West Ter's
(not in D – Newfoundland)

[2:122  blank]

[2:123]
Canada (See Enc: Brit
New Ed: Vol 4

—

Area equal to the whole of Europe

—

 Population 1880   ~~abt~~ ~~5,000,000?~~ ~~nearly~~ 4 to 5 million

Timber
principal timber, white and red pine – the woods are full of white oak, elm,
beech, ash, maple (bird's eye, curled, &c.) walnut, cedar, birch, ~~and~~
tamarac, ~~black walnut, bird's eye and.~~ ~~Maple~~ Sugar ~~groves~~ orchards,
(maple)

[2:124  blank]

[2:125]
the honey-bee everywhere – rural ponds and lakes, (often abounding with
the great white sweet-smelling water-lily) – wild fruits and berries everywhere – in the vast flat grounds, the prairie-anemone

[2:126  blank]

[2:127]

Canada
The Fisheries of Canada are almost unparallelled. The seal, the sturgeon,
the finest salmon, white fish, cod, haddock, mackerel, herring
the immense area, and the varieties of waters – the Lakes, the St Lawrence, the adjacencies of Newfoundland and Nova Scotia on the east, – in
fact all the way from Davis Straits to Halifax – and the equally rich region
on the Pacific side, (on this   [the Pacific ?] ~~latter~~ side great oyster beds)

[2:128  blank]

[2:129]
Then furs, deer-skins, and those of the bear, ~~buffalo~~ wolf, beaver, fox

(all ~~vario~~ sorts) otter, coon, mink, martin, ~~and buffalo~~ musk-rat, &c.
Grains in following order
Wheat
Barley
Rye
Oats
Indian Corn

[2:130 blank]

[2:131]

1

If the most significant ~~modern~~ trait of modern civilization is benevo-
lence, (as a leading statesman has said,) it is doubtful whether ~~it~~ this is any-
where illustrated to a fuller degree than in ~~this~~ the province of Ontario. All
the maimed, ~~needy~~ insane, idiotic blind, ~~and~~ deaf and dumb needy sick and
old, minor criminals, fallen women, foundlings have advanced and ample
provision of ~~land an~~ house and care and oversight, at least fully equal to
anything of the kind in

[2:132 blank]

[2:133]

2

any of the United States – probably indeed superior to them. Of Ontario
For its eighty-eight electoral ridings, each one returning a member of parlia-
ment ~~of population the Province has~~ there are four Insane Asylums, an Idiot
Asylum ~~a Blind~~ an one

[2:134 blank]

[2:135]
3                                    Gal 12 [not WW's hand]
[institution for the Blind, one for the Deaf and Dumb, one for Foundlings,
a Reformatory for Girls, one for Women, and no end of homes for the old
and infirm, for waifs, and for the Sick.

[2:136]
encl                         [very rough notes in WW's hand]
better elast
How narrow

Xxxxx Getting in the
dincian [ ? ] in Rome one afternoon
xxxxx found xxxxx
[gr]oup of little girls,
also " (xxx robber,
~~xxxxxxxx~~

4                                                        [2:137]

Its School System, founded on the Massachusetts plan, is one of the best
and most comprehensive in the world.

~~The~~ Some of the good people of Ontario have complained ~~to me~~ in my
hearing of ~~om omis~~ faults and fraudulencies, ~~on~~ commissive and omissive, on
the part of their government, but I guess ~~they~~ said people have reason to
bless their stars at the general fairness, economy, wisdom and liberality
of their officers and administration

[2:138 blank]

[2:139]

'80   Canada[3423]

Aug 21 [London] – I rose this morning at 4 and look'd out on the most
pure and refulgent starry show. Right over my head ~~head was~~ like a Tree-
Universe Spreading with its orb-apples — Aldebaran leading the Hyades. —
~~High, too,~~ Jupiter of amazing lustre, softness and volume — and not far
behind heavy Saturn — both past the meridian — The ~~Pleiades like~~ seven
~~dazzling Sp~~ Sparkling gems of the Pleiades. ~~due over me.~~ The full moon,
voluptuous and yellow, ~~but~~ and full of radiance, an hour to setting in

[2:140  blank]

[2:141]

the west. Every thing so fresh, so still, the delicious something there is in
early youth, in early dawn – the spirit, the spring, the _feel_, the air and light,
precursors of the untried Sun, ~~life,~~ love, action, forenoon, noon, life – ~~and~~
~~yet~~ full-fibred ~~of~~ latent with them all. —

---

3423. This date and word are omitted in the published version, the diary portion of
which ends with the two paragraphs dealing with Aug. 21 and Aug. 29. After this, the editor
has a notation: "[Elsewhere in this diary he writes of 'the long clear quaver of the robin, its
mellow and reedy note,' although he erased the words as being unsatisfactory. But I think
they are admirably descriptive of the timbre of the robin's evening song as well as the song
itself.]"

And is not that Orion ~~the~~ mighty hunter ~~up there~~? Are not those the three glittering studs in his belt? ~~There~~ And there to the north Capella & his kids.

[2:142 blank]

[2:143]

### Canada – at Dr B's

Aug 29 '80

– the ~~groups~~ robins on the grassy lawn, (I sometimes see a dozen at a time, great fat fellows) — the little black-and-yellow bird [the goldfinch] with his billowy flight – the ~~groups~~ flocks of sparrows –

[2:144 blank]

[2:145]

Birds in Ontario
        talk with Wm Saunders[3424]

lark-sparrow – sings
/robins                       July
/black birds (3 kinds)    1880
/cat bird
/rice-bird (bob-o-link)
/thrush
/blue-bird
 cuckoo
 sand-piper
⎧ night-hawk,   (nearly allied
⎨ (my hawk)        to whippoorwill)
⎩    same as night-jar
 wren
 blue-jay
 king-fisher

3424. Most of the rest of the MS from here on, except for the paragraph of two sentences, beginning "Walt Whitman is at Ha-ha bay," and the paragraph on *Aug* 1 [1880], is omitted in the published version. Both of these appear earlier in the *Diary in Canada.*

The Feinberg Collection MS, on which *Walt Whitman's Diary in Canada* is based, ends here. The rest of the material in the book edited by Kennedy, sub-headed "From Other Journals of Walt Whitman" and referred to on the title-page by the phrase "With Extracts from Other of His Diaries and Literary Note-Books," occupies pp. 49–73 in the published version. In the present collection, however, it is printed as footnotes in its appropriate place by date, even though its MS is not in the Feinberg Collection. Most of it dates between 1878 and 1885, and thus it seems best to use it along with *Daybook* entries.

wood-pecker
high-hole

[2:146]

write your name please
Mary Ettie Lorenzen    [not in Whitman's hand]
          T h r e e
     R a d i a t i o n s
     ? ~~of Songs~~
        & Songs left over

[2:147]

Shore-lark (northern bird)
all the Sparrows,
Oriole (hanging bird – golden robin)
Scarlet tanager (common here)
Meadow-lark
yellow-bird
purple martin
Swallows (go South August & Sept)
cedar-bird (very common)

[2:148]

          Tuesday forenoon July 6th 80
— A beautiful calm summer forenoon, as we sit here (M E L and myself) on the verandah of Dr Bucke's house – the pleasant view, ~~the~~ the wheat
& & hay fields, the birds singing, the sun shining, in ~~a~~ the pleasant breeze,
and all.
     Nature ~~so~~/so perfect.

[2:149]

the elm, the maple, the locust, ~~the~~ mountain ash, tamarack and oak

[2:150 blank]

[2:151]

Trinity Rock and Cape Eternity two indescribable
a good deal of cord wood, appears to be mostly white birch

[2:152]

Walt Whitman is ~~stopping~~ at Ha-ha bay. ~~on the Saguenay river.~~ He ~~says~~ ~~thinks~~ says he would like to spend a month every year of his life ~~amid that~~ there on the Saguenay river, and near Cape Eternity and Trinity Rock

[2:153  blank]

[2:154  blank]

[2:155]

Canada July & Aug: '80

Started from London 8.40 a m. July 26
    by RR to Toronto – arrived
      in T. same day.
left Toronto by steamboat
    Algerian        July 27
arrived at Kingston 5 a m  "  28
Stopt at Dr W G Metcalf's
down at the Thousand Islands
    three days – "Hub Island"
left Kingston  6 a m  Aug 3
arrived at Montreal same evening
left Montreal      Aug 5
  down to Quebec in steamer
        Montreal
left Quebec 7 a m  Aug 6 in
  steamer Saguenay
Aug 6  down the St Lawrence
      splendid scenery
  & night of 6th
7th Up the Saguenay to Chicoutimi
  & Ha-ha bay – Cape Eternity
    & Trinity Rock
  – then down, and, on our return
Aug 8 early a m arrived in Quebec
  Staid two days
Aug 10 early a m in Montreal

[2:156]

Walt Whitman is ~~living~~ at Quebec, delighted with the queer old French city, making ~~daily~~ leisurely explorations among the old places, the churches, the hilly streets, the Citadel, and the environs. He specially admires, all through the province, ~~the numbers perpetual sight of pretty towns and villages~~ after ~~you~~ passing the mouth of the Ottawa, going east, the perpetual recurrence of pretty towns & villages along the St L   For ~~over a hu~~ two hundred miles, the white clusters are repeated ~~over & over~~ continually or in groups, nestling in trees & orchards near the water, each with its glistening church ~~spir~~ spire or tower high in the middle of the town

[2:157]

Aug 10   left Montreal in
    Algerian – had a pleasant
    voyage (two days & nights
       to Toronto —
Aug 12 arr: in Toronto by
    Algerian – 3 hours at Queen's
      hotel   left 11 a m
Aug 12   arrived in Hamilton
   13 ⎫
   14 ⎬ in Hamilton
[Back home in London Aug. 14]
    (Collate the above with one at beginning of diary) [not in WW's hand]

[2:158–159]
[Railroad map of parts of Ontario, Quebec, Michigan, Ohio, Pennsylvania, New York, Vermont, Massachusetts, and Connecticut, with:]

## DISTANCE CARD
—

#### MILES.

| | | |
|---|---|---:|
| Niagara Falls to Toronto | ...... | 84 |
| Toronto to Montreal | .......... | 370 |
| Montreal to Quebec | ........... | 180 |
| " | to Portland | 297 |
| " | to New York | 403 |
| " | to Albany | 261 |
| " | to Troy | 256 |
| " | to White Mountains | 76 |
| " | to Saratoga | 212 |
| " | to Cleveland | 712 |
| " | to Pittsburg | 851 |

"      to  Boston  . . . . . . . . . .  334
"      to  Cincinnati  . . . . . . .  967
"      to  Louisville  . . . . . . . . .1104
"      to  St.  Louis  . . . . . . . . .1325
"      to  New  Orleans  . . . . . .2504
Portland  to  Boston  . . . . . . . . . .  168
Saratoga  to  New  York  . . . . . . . . .  187
New  York  to  Philadelphia  . . . . .  88
Philadelphia  to  Baltimore  . . . . . .  98
Baltimore  to  Washington  . . . . . .  40
Ogdensburg  to  Ottawa  . . . . . . . .  53

[2:160]

Lakes of the Thousand Islands
          St Lawrence river – Aug 1
I write this in the ~~b~~ most beautiful, extensive region of lakes and islands
one can probably see on earth – have been here several days, leisurely cruising
around – ~~We~~ Came down ~~here two or th days ago, an cruising around~~ in a
handsome little steam-yacht which I am living on half the time – the ~~w~~ lakes
are very extensive (over 1000 square miles) & the islands numberless, some
small  some large. Here and there dotted with summer villas. I am pretty
well. Go ~~to~~ on to Montreal Tuesday, 3$^d$,  (to Elmer rec'd your letter) ~~and~~
so down the St L
Pete
Elmer
Mont        Lou
~~Dave Moore~~
Eugene Crosby
Al Johnston

[2:161]

[Pictures of Cape Trinity and Ha Ha Bay.]

[2:162  blank]

[2:163]

Montreal to Quebec    Aug 5–10

[2:164]

Dr J M Drake

[2:165  blank]

Miscellaneous Journals

<u>Wednesday, 4th March, 1863.</u> Scene up to Noon. Close of the 37th Congress; House. Well, here is the 4th of March, and two out of the four years of the Lincoln administration have gone by. And now there are two to follow. What will happen during those two years?

<u>Forenoon, 4th March</u>. The House now presents a most animated and characteristic scene. The ranges of crowded galleries are in shadow, while the strong day showers its powerful and steady streams upon the floor. Did I think and say it looked so much better at night? Well, I think I never saw it look better than now (11¼ A.M.).

A member from New York has just been making a most excited little speech. At this moment the clerk is calling the ayes and noes. The members and many distinguished and undistinguished visitors are filling the floor, talking, walking, sauntering in twoes or threes, or gathered together in little knots. — The clapping of hands calling the pages; the fresh green of the carpets and desks; the strong, good-tinted panel frames of the glass roof; the short, decided voice of the speaker; the continual soda-pop-like burstings of members calling "Mr. Speaker! Mr. Speaker!" the incessant bustle, motion, surging hubbub of voices, undertoned but steady.

There is a rather notable absence of military uniforms on the floor of the house; crowded as it is at the moment, I do not, as I sweep my eyes around, see a single shoulder-strap.

Interruption: a message from the Senate of the United States; it is half-past eleven; there are but thirty minutes left for the 37th Congress; the ladies' gallery in the House is about half of the whole room devoted to the public; a resolution is adopted giving a boy who was employed by the House $100 — he has had his ankles crushed, disabled; the hands of the clock move on; there is great hubbub and confusion, actual disorder; bang! bang! bang!

the speaker's hammer is rapidly falling, and he sternly calls for gentlemen to come to order; and still the hands of the clock invisibly move on; there are but fifteen minutes left; voices of hubbub; bump, bump, bump, bump, bump! "Gentlemen will please take their seats." "Not one step further, gentlemen, till there is something like order."

Five minutes to twelve; there is a kind of hush and abeyance — not the hubbub now there has been; some filibustering is attempted on a small scale; tellers are called to clear up a disputed vote; the strong hum goes on; the crowd is very great; the laws of the door have been relaxed and everybody appears to have somebody in tow; the hands are on 12; the speaker rises; the clerks, officers, pages, gather in a close phalanx around the desk, on the steps and close to them; the hubbub subsides into the stillness of death; the doorkeepers guard all the doors; the speaker's address. — The 37th Congress is adjourned *sine die;* the impression evidently good as he concludes; there is hearty applause, and then things are untied; the doors fly open; the manydrest public streams in; all below there is now a crawling jam of people, — soldier boys, hoosiers, gents, etc. etc. etc. A dust arises from the tread of so many footsteps — boots with the mud dried on them; the last breath of the 37th Congress, full of dim opaque particles, rises and fills the air of the most beautiful room in the world; but the light strikes down through it; the crowd wave their hats.

VICTOR HUGO's ANNÉE TERRIBLE [1870–71] (as translated to me by Mr. Aubin, Oct. '72). First the Prologue, the splendid portraiture of the People and the Mob. A whole world, if it is wrong, does not outweigh one just man. Distinction between the People and the Mob — magnificent. It is not incense that has broken the nose of the Sphinx: it is the bosom made vulgar by the belly. — "SEDAN." The close, where the sword of France representing all the great heroic characters and all the famous victories (mentioned by name) is "by the hand of a bandit" ignominiously surrendered.

[The passages in "L'Année Terrible" referred to are as follows:

"Un monde, s'il a tort, ne pèse pas un juste,
Tout un océan fou bat en vain un grand cœur."]

Says Hugo: The crowd and the idealist have rude encounters: Moses, Ezekiel, Dante, were men grave and severe. The spirit of redoutable thinkers can be better employed than in caressing the sphinx —

"Ce grand monstre de pierre accroupé qui médite,
Ayant en lui l'énigme adorable ou maudite;

L'ouragan n'est pas tendre aux colosses émus;
C'est ne pas d'encensoirs que le sphinx est camus.
La vérité, voilà le grand encens austère
Qu'on doit à cette masse où palpite un mystère,
Et qui porte en son sein qu'un ventre appesantit,
Le droit juste mêlé de l'injuste appétit."

At the close of the section called "Août" and also headed "Sedan," Hugo is describing in grandiose imagery the battle of Sedan, — the vast clouds of smoke, the thunder-roll of the cannon, the feeling of honor, of devotion to country, the sublime moment when, in the passion of battle, the soldier is ready to consecrate his life to his country's welfare, when the trumpets are breathing their thrilling sounds, and the word is "resist or die!" And then (continues Hugo) is heard this monstrous and cowardly cry "I wish to live," "Je veux vivre" (alluding to Napoleon the Little).

"Alors la Gaule, alors la France, alors la gloire,
Alors Brennus, l'audace, et Clovis, la victoire,

. . . . . . . . . . . . . . .

Les hommes du dernier carré de Waterloo,
Et tous les chefs de guerre, Héristal, Charlemagne,

. . . . . . . . . . . . . . .

Napoleón plus grand que César et Pompée
Par la main d'un bandit rendirent leur épée."] [3424a]

---

3424a.  These two journal entries, on Congress and on Victor Hugo, are printed in the "Other Journals" section of *Walt Whitman's Diary in Canada,* pp. 49–54.

## Autobiographical Notes

All through young and middle age I thought my heredity-stamp was mainly decidedly from my mother's side; but, as I grow older, and latent traits come out, I see my father's also. As to loving and disinterested parents, no boy or man ever had more cause to bless and thank them than I.[3425]

---

Like the Whitmans, the Van Velsors too were farmers on their own land. Though both families were well-to-do for those times, the biblical prayer for "neither poverty nor riches" might have been considered as fulfilled in either case. The poet's father died in Brooklyn, New York, July 11, 1855; the "dear dear mother" in Camden, New Jersey, May 23, 1873 ... Though the concrete and entire foundation of the poet, as person and writer, doubtless comes from his solid English fatherhood, the emotional and liberty-loving, the social, the preponderating qualities of adhesiveness, immovable gravitation and simplicity, with a certain conservative protestantism and other traits, are unmistakably from his motherhood, and are pure Hollandic or Dutch.[3426]

---

Going back far enough ancestrally, Walt Whitman undoubtedly comes meandering from a blended tri-heredity stream of Dutch (Hollandisk), the original Friends (Quakers), and the Puritans of Cromwell's time. The first Whitman immigrant settled in Connecticut, 1635, and a son of his went over to Long Island as farmer at West Hills, Suffolk County; and a young descendant five generations afterward marries a daughter of Cornelius and Amy Van Velsor (the last of Quaker training and *née* Williams). This daughter was the mother of W. W. Though developed, and Anglofied, and

3425. This paragraph, the first in the section called "Personal Memoranda Notes and Jottings" in *Walt Whitman's Diary in Canada* (Boston, 1904), p. 66, is — according to its editor, William Sloane Kennedy — written on the back of a letter, dated 15 October 1883, from James M. Scovel (see footnote 71, above).

3426. According to W. S. Kennedy, who used this paragraph in *Walt Whitman's Diary in Canada,* pp. 66–67, "For Dr. Bucke's *Walt Whitman* the poet sent on certain autobiographic materials in his own autograph. The [above] paragraph was not used by Dr. Bucke."

Americanized, she was Hollandisk from top to toe, and W. W. inherits her to the life, emotionally, full-bloodedness, voice, and physiognomy.

Whitman favors (as the old vernacular word had it) his mother, *née* Louisa Van Velsor, of Queens County, New York. She was of ordinary medium size (a little *plus*), of splendid physique and health, a hard worker, had eight children, was beloved by all who met her; good-looking to the last; lived to be nearly eighty. No tenderer or more invariable tie was ever between mother and son than the love between her and W. W. No one could have seen her and her father, Major Kale (Cornelius) Van Velsor, either in their prime or in their older age, without instantly perceiving their plainly marked Hollandisk physiognomy, color, and body-build. Walt Whitman has all of it: he shows it in his old features now, his full flesh and red color. The Van Velsors (Walt's mother's family) were pure Low Dutch of the third and fourth remove from the original emigrants. Few realize how this Dutch element has percolated into our New York, Pennsylvania, and other regions,[3427] not so much in ostensible literature and politics, but deep in the blood and breed of the race, and to tinge all that is to come. Like the Quakers, the Dutch are very practical and materialistic, and are great money-makers, in the bulk and concrete of the ostent of life, but are yet terribly transcendental and cloudy, too. More than half the Hollandisk immigrants to New York Bay became farmers, and a goodly portion of the rest became engineers or sailors.

It is curious how deep influences, elements, and characteristic-trends operate through races and long periods of time, in practical events and palpably in long continued struggles of war and peace — and then sprout out eventually in some marked book, perhaps poem. Whitman himself is fond of resuming the history and development of the Low Dutch, and their fierce war against Philip and Alva, and the building of the dykes, and the shipping and trade and colonization from 1600 to the present, and the old cities and towers and soldiery and markets and salt-air, and flat topography, and human physiognomy and bodily form (not the Jewish seems to be more strictly perpetuated than these Hollandisk), and their coming and planting here in America, and investing themselves not so much in outward manifestations, but in the blood and deeds of the race; and the poet considers his "Leaves of Grass" to be, in some respects, spinally understood only by reference to that Hollandisk history and personality.[3428]

3427. W. S. Kennedy writes in *Walt Whitman's Diary in Canada*, p. 69n: "See other details of this in my *Reminiscences of Walt Whitman*, p. 89.

3428. In a notation preceding this material, W. S. K. says: "For my work on Whitman (the bulk of which he read in MS. and approved), he sent me the following notes on his ancestry. I used a small portion of these, inserting what seemed available almost verbatim, but give them now entire" (*Walt Whitman's Diary in Canada*, pp. 67–70, for the note and passage).

I became acquainted with Mr Whitman in 1884 when I bought and moved in the little home 328 Mickle street, within three doors of which I lived. ~~The~~ We boys had a quoit club, and W. made us a present of a handsome set of quoits for pitching. He had a kind word for us all, and we all liked him, though I thought then and have ∧^since been confirmed in it, that there was a good deal of dignity and even reserve, in his manners, with all their cordiality

^drifted
He had ~~come~~ to Camden in the summer of 1873, seriously ill with paral-
~~He ha~~
ysis, and ~~fo~~ for nearly three years remained very low and broken down, the result of overstrained labors down in the ~~War~~ Secession war. In 1876 he began open-air treatment and rest down in ~~th~~ a county farm-house, on Timber Creek, in Camden county, New Jersey, and spent the summers there for several years, and part of the winters also. He describes it all in his book, Specimen Days. The result was favorable, and he grew stronger. But he was always lame and disabled.

I have thus given a few brief notes of my year with Mr W[hitman]
    as he is        Among his
Probably few have had a better chance to know him ∧ in reality. ~~His~~ main traits are patience, ~~gr~~ good nature, and a sunny disposition. He is not religious in the usual sense. I never knew him to have prayer or say grace at meals, nor did he go to church at all. He ~~always~~ gave freely to the poor, and helped
indigent                                        fuel or
many∧old persons and widows constantly, sometimes with food or∧money, sometimes paying the rent. With ~~a~~ great frankness and naturalness he was entirely free from indelicacy or any unchastity ~~in any form~~ whatever
                                                He
some
had∧spells of sickness, more ·or less severe, but while I was with him was
            around
well enough to be ~~about~~ the house or get out with a little assistance. He employed himself six or seven hours every day reading or writing. He was pretty tall, close on six feet high, weighed over 200 pounds, was full-blooded, had generally a good appetite, and slept pretty soundly. He knew almost
                            wonderfully
everybody, was fond of visitors, and was ~~liked~~ popular among ~~yo~~ men and women, young and old. He always gave me good advice and help, and was the best friend I ever had.[3429]

There is something in concrete Nature itself in all its parts that is a quality, an identity, apart from and superior to any appreciation of the same through realism or mysticism (the very thought of which involves abstraction) or through literature or art. This something belonging to the objects themselves not only lies beyond all expressions of literature and art, but seems disdainful of them and fades away at their touch.[3430]

After reading the pages of *Specimen Days* do you object that they are a great jumble, everything scattered, disjointed, bound together without coherence, without order or system? My answer would be, So much the better do they reflect the life they are intended to stand for.

Though I would not have dared to gather the various pieces of the following book in a single volume with a generic name unless I felt the strong inward thread of spinality running through all the pieces and giving them affinity-purpose — I yet realize that the collection is indeed a mélange and its cohesion and singleness of purpose not so evident at first glance.[3431]

It is said, perhaps rather quizzically, by my friends that I bring civilization, politics, the topography of a country, and even the hydrography, to one final test, — the capability of producing, favoring, and maintaining a fine crop of children, a magnificent race of men and women. I must confess I look with comparative indifference on all the lauded triumphs of the greatest manufacturing, exporting, gold-and-silver-producing nation in comparison with a race of really fine physical perfectionists.[3432]

Col. J. W. F[orney] remarked in the course of our talk this evening: "If I were asked to put my finger on the name of any eminent official in this great city [Philadelphia] — and I know nine-tenths of them — as of undoubted honesty and integrity, I could not do it." (F., who has been in public life for forty years, and knows everybody, especially the Philadelphians, is not

3429. This material is from a MS in Whitman's hand in the Feinberg Collection, although it was obviously meant to be used by someone else, in this case William H. Duckett, a young man who stayed for a time at 328 Mickle Street in the mid-1880s and had to be sued for his board by Mrs Mary Davis, Whitman's housekeeper (see footnote 2687 and numerous other places in the *Daybook*). It is thought that Duckett tried to sell this passage and some others he wrote to Dr R. M. Bucke: see the full story in William White, "Billy Duckett: Whitman Rogue," *American Book Collector*, XXI (February 1971), 20–23, which reprints the material above.

3430. From *Walt Whitman's Diary in Canada*, p. 70, with a comment by W. S. Kennedy that the MS. was marked in red ink; "? a ¶ for Specimen Days."

3431. From *Walt Whitman's Diary in Canada*, pp. 70–71, with a comment by W. S. Kennedy that the MS. was marked: "2d vol. Specimen Days."

3432. From *Walt Whitman's Diary in Canada*, in the section of "Personal Memoranda Notes and Jottings," p. 71.

a sour man, either — is quite lenient, human, tolerant.) [Col. Forney died in 1881.][3433]

---

In modern times the new word *Business* has been brought to the front and now dominates individuals and nations (always of account in all ages, but never before confessedly leading the rest as in our 19th century): Business — not the mere sordid, prodding, muck-and-money-raking mania, but an immense and noble attribute of man, the occupation of nations and individuals (without which is no happiness), the progress of the masses, the tie and interchange of all peoples of the earth. Ruthless war and arrogant dominion-conquest was the ideal of the antique and mediaeval hero; Business shall be, nay is, the word of the modern hero.[3434]

---

[1883.]   Meeting with Thurlow Weed and long talk with him.[3435]

---

3433. From *Walt Whitman's Diary in Canada,* in the section of "Personal Memoranda Notes and Jottings," p. 72; there is no date, though the first reference to Col. Forney in the *Daybook* is 15 October 1877 (see footnote 193 for a brief summary of their relationship).
   3434. With a heading by W. S. Kennedy, "Notes for a Canada Lecture, never delivered," this passage is printed in *Walt Whitman's Diary in Canada,* pp. 72–73.
   3435. From *Walt Whitman's Diary in Canada,* p. 73. W. S. Kennedy dates the sentence 1883, though there is no mention of Weed in the *Daybook* anywhere or the *Correspondence*; and the year must be wrong as Weed, an important New York politician and editor of the Albany *Evening Journal,* died in 1882 at the age of 85.

# The Primer Of Words

For American

For American Young Men and Women !

For Literats !

Orators', readers,

Musicians,

Judges, Presidents &c

Words[3436]

[Inside front cover]

[Clipping:]

It is estimated that there are 587 languages and general dialects in Europe, 937 in Asia, 226 in Africa, and 1,263 in America, in all nearly 3,000.

The Virtues

Knowledge       Courage

Health          Charity

Activity        Cleanliness

Domus, a house — hence domestic

[Clipping:]

THE HON. GEO. P. MARSH, in a recent lecture on the English language, says

3436. Sometime after 1856 Whitman cut out most of the pages of a book and kept in the stubs so that he could tip in sheets of paper, left over green wrappers from the first (1855) *Leaves of Grass,* City of Williamsburgh unused tax forms, endpapers from the second (1856) *Leaves,* and other sheets and scraps of various colors. On these he wrote notes on grammar, language, phrases, and words, some from French — all of which he apparently intended to use as sort of a dictionary of the English language, a subject that obsessed him all of his adult life, showing up in his poetry and in much that he wrote: see, for example, *An American Primer,* edited by Horace Traubel after Whitman's death (Boston: Small, Maynard & Company, 1904) — which text is also reprinted in the present volume, below. Whitman intended to call this book "The Primer of Words: For American Young Men and Women, For Literats, Orators, Teachers, Musicians, Judges, Presidents, &c."; and another instance of his attitude toward language is the paragraph Whitman wrote on the first page of this home-made word book, *Words,* and which is quoted in full above under Whitman's heading "Grammar." This 294-page notebook, here reproduced in type from the MS in the Feinberg Collection, Library of Congress, has on the front cover and on the spine two small paper labels, on which is written in Whitman's hand: "Words." This is the title given this section of the *Daybooks and Notebooks of Walt Whitman,* published in this edition of *The Collected Writings of Walt Whitman* for the first time in its entirety. The pages are not numbered in the MS, but I have supplied numbers, which are printed here within square brackets. In addition to Whitman's holograph material, I have also included most of his clippings from newspapers, magazines, and books, especially as much of it has to do with language, words, and grammar; though not written by him, he most likely would have printed it if he had ever completed his dictionary project.

that the English words found in use by good writers hardly fall short of 100,000. Even if a man was able on extraordinary occasions to bring into use half of that number, he generally contented himself with far fewer. Each individual used in his daily life a repertory of words to some extent peculiar to himself. Few scholars used as many as 10,000 English words; ordinary people not more than 3,000. In all Shakespeare there were not more than 15,000 words; in all Milton, 8,000. Of the Egyptian hieroglyphics there were but 800, and it was said that the vocabulary of the Italian opera was scarcely greater.

[Clipping:]

The English Government has started the word "telegram" for telegraph dispatch. A correspondent discusses the propriety thereof and writes: An epig*ram,* a diag*ram,* a monog*ram,* and an anag*ram* — but, an autogra*ph,* a lithogra*ph,* a photogra*ph,* and a telegra*ph.* What is the principle? When the compound denotes the character of the writing, it takes *gram;* when it denotes the means, it takes *graph.* In the case of a telegraphic message, the means of transmission are indicated. Therefore the proper word is telegra*ph.* Do not be misled by Government "telegram" — an illustration of the proverb, that a little learning is a dangerous thing.

Webster's Dictionary
Prefaces

On English Language, from
70 to 80,000 words
Or rather, (same authority, about
100,000 words

[Front flyleaf]

Ethnic — heathen
pot sherds — broken pieces pot
euphuism — (of the time
of Elizabeth)

[Several lines illegible]

pessimist (a universal complainer
(the reverse of optimist

[Verso of front flyleaf]

[Clipping:]

DAYS BEFORE BOOKS.—In the old ignorant times, before women were read-ers, the history was handed down from mother to daughter, &c., and William of Malmesbury picked up his history, from the time of Venerable Bede to his time, out of old songs, for there was no writer in England from Bede to him. So my nurse had the history from the Conquest down to Charles I. in ballad. Before printing, Old Wives' Tales were ingenious; and since printing came in fashion, till a little before the Civil Wars, the ordinary sort of people were not taught to read. Now-a-days, books are common, and most of the poor people understand letters; and the many good books and variety of turns of affairs, have put all the old fables out of doors. And the divine art of print-ing and gunpowder have frightened away Robin Good-fellow and the fairies. —AUBREY.

[1: blue Williamsburgh tax form:]
## Grammar.

Drawing language into line by rigid grammatical rules, is the theory of the martinet applied to the most ethereal processes of the spirit, and to the luxurant growth of all that makes art.— It is for small school-masters, not for great souls. — Not only the Dictionary of the English Language, but the Grammar of it, has yet to be written. —

[2: blank]

[3: Williamsburgh tax form:]
All through, a common gender ending in ist as —

> lovist     both
> hatist     masc
>           &
>           fem
>
> — hater    m
> hatress   f   &c

[4: blank]

[5: Williamsburgh tax form:]
## Murray's Grammar

The fault principally that he fails to understand to where those points where the language [is] strongest, and where [the] developements should [be] most encouraged, namely, in being <u>elliptic</u> and <u>idiomatic</u>. — Murray would make of the young men merely a correct and careful set of writers under laws. — He would deprive writing of its life — there would be nothing voluntary and insociant left. —

[6: blank]

[7: Williamsburgh tax form:]
as [?], punctuation marks, were not extant in old writings or inscriptions — they were commenced about (1520) three hundred years ago.

[8: blank]

[9: white sheet:]
Mácrocosm (as ensemble) – (from Greek) The great whole world, in
     opposition to the part that comes in minute experience. —
                     — more large indefinute

---

Mícrocosm – the world of man – (? the little world concentred in
     man) Man as an epitome of all — (more definite)

---

Hél=lé=nés

---

riffacciamento – rumble (sort of mosaic work mixture mess –

[8a: blank]

[9a: green sheet:]
[Clipping:]

### THE ANGLO-SAXON RACE.

In 1620 the Anglo-Saxon race numbered about 6,000,000, and was confined to England, Wales, and Scotland: and the combination of which it is the result was not then more than half perfected, for neither Wales nor Scotland was half-Saxonised at the time. Now it numbers 60,000,000 of human beings, planted upon all the islands and continents of the earth, and increasing everywhere by an immense ratio of progression. It is fast absorbing or displacing all the sluggish races or barbarous tribes of men that have occupied the continents of Americà, Africa, Asia, and the islands of the ocean. If no great physical revolution supervene to check its propagation, it will number 800,-000,000 of human beings in less than 150 years from the present time — all speaking the same language, centered to the same literature and religion, and exhibiting all its inherent and inalienable characteristics. Thus the population of the earth is fast becoming Anglo-Saxonised by blood. But the English language is more self-expansive and aggresive than the blood of that race. When a community begins to speak the English language it is half – Saxonised, even if not a drop of Anglo-Saxon blood runs in its veins. Ireland was never colonised from England like North America or Australia, but nearly the whole of its 7,000,000 or 8,000,000, already speak the English language, which is the preparatory state to being entirely absorbed into the Anglo-Saxon race, as one of its most vigorous and useful elements. Everywhere the English language is gaining upon the languages of the earth, and preparing those who speak for this absorption. The young generation of the East Indies is learning it; and it is probable that within fifty years 65,000,000 of human beings of the Asiatic race will speak the language on that continent. So it is in the United States. About 50,000 emigrants from Germany and other countries of continental Europe are arriving in this country every year. Perhaps they cannot speak a word of English when they first land on our shores; but in the course of a few years they master the language to some extent. Their children sit upon the same benches in our common schools with those of native Americans, and become, as they grow up and diffuse themselves among the rest of the population, completely Anglo-Saxonised. Thus the race is fast occupying, and subduing to its genius, all the continents and islands of the earth. The grandson of many a young man who reads these lines ·will probably live to see the day when that race will number its 800,000,000 of human beings. Their unity, harmony, and brotherhood must be determined by the relations between Great Britain and the United States. Their union will be the union of the two worlds. If they discharge their duty to each other and to mankind, they must become the united heart of the mighty race they represent, feeding its myriad veins with the blood of moral and political life. Upon the state of their fellowship, then, more than upon the union of any two nations on earth, depends the well-being of humanity, and the peace and progress of the world.

imbroglio, a mixed up mess of troubles

Did he ~~dit~~ do it a purpose?

That's so, easy enough. —

That's a sick ticket

Well I was looking for a man – about your size

"go back" — "go back on him"

---

He works on his own ~~k~~ hook

---

a good American word    centurion

---

Kosmos,   noun masculine or feminine, a person who[se] scope of mind, or
    whose range in a particular science, includes all, the whole known
    universe

[10: blank]

[11: white sheet, small:]
There should be could easily be a dictionary made of words fit to be used in
in an English (American) opera, — or for vocal-lyric purposes, songs, ballads,
recitatives, &c.

[12: written upside down:]
ed by some that the ~~democracy~~ human     down in the act of These

[13: white sheet, very small:]
    "Words"    the New York Bowery boy — "Sa-a-y!"

What – a – t ?

[14: blank]

[15: green sheet (unused covers for the binding of the first [1855] edition of
*Leaves of Grass*) with a strip of white paper pasted on it:]
all right                    "So long"
swim out                    — (a delicious American – New York –
cave in                        idiomatic phrase at parting
~~dry up~~    dry up            equivalent to "good bye"
        switch off            "adieu"    &c
— git and git
he is }
I am } on that
"hold up your head up."
"Bully for you"
a "nasty" man.

"that's rough."
log – rolling
may–be (mebbee)
bub
sis      honey–fugling.

---

~~Guau~~ – Guacho [wá̆ – ko]
give him away

[16: blank]

[17: small pale blue sheet:]
   ⌊ Words ⌋
Empiricism – as an acquaintance with a number of isolated facts, yet not of
       the subtle relation and bearing of them, the meaning – their part in
       the ensemble – ~~their~~ the instinct of what they prove. —

---

☞   Modern sense of the term
   simply the direct facts, by rote, without grasping the spirit, the real
   meaning of them.

[18: blank]

[19: green sheet:]
Sachem            passim
wardance         (every where
powwow,           here and there,
Moundbuilders,    used as a word
Mohekan          of reference.)
prairie,

---

"on the stump"
    (from the western practice at times, of political speakers mounting a
    tree–stump, ~~for their~~ and so holding forth

---

barracoon – collection of slaves
        in Africa, or anywhere
      ("I see the slave barracoon")

---

    collaborateurs
? co–laborers
   ? co-laboraters

[20: blank]

[21: Williamsburgh tax form, clipped:]
Is it not self-proved that the African (? & Asiatic) hieroglyphs are more
ancient than the phonetic sounds of the Phenician letters. —        Yes,
it seems clearly so to me

[22: blank]

[23: Williamsburgh tax form, clipped:]
Alphabetic letters introduced into Europe   1500 B. C.
viz: Phenician letters, by Cadmus, into Greece.
– facts veiled in the vapory tradition of

[24: blank]

[25: Williamsburgh tax form:]
   desideratum – Sound–Marks.
One of the first desiderata [is] a font of type, in a Dictiona[ry] [ ? ] in
printed composition [an]y-how, is a set of arbitra[ry] sound–marks attached to letters [,] each mark belonging to that specific sound. — How
clear this would make language! especially to a child, an illiter[ate] [r]eader
aloud, or a foreigner
leg is la tive

---

O "Voltaire, Montesquieu, Jean–Jacques Rousseau, Buffon, and Diderot,
— all the genius of the French tongue is to be found in the style of those five
writers."
                          Arsene Houssaye.
                              1850

[26: blank]

[27: green sheet:]
Feuilleton                    Attache
Feuilletonist                 at – a – sha
regime                        one attached to any person, establish-
                                  ment, or what not.

vis–a–viz, face to face   opposite, person seated opposite

---

       noun              viser v  n     to take aim
visee —        vi za – aim, end, object
                   — to aim at

vidette

___

genre        ja (zhän–r)        peculiar to that person, period or place
                                — not universal

___

accroupie     (Venus accroupie)
Ma femme     ("She is mine — ma femme")
parvenu
forte – (strong –

___

                (I prefer dilletant
dilletante     singular     and
dilletanti     pl          "dilletants"

finale
col–pŏr–teŭr                (peddler)

largesse              arriere:
                           behind

petit

[28: blank]

[29: green sheet:]
Martinet
~~chaff       "The omnibus man chaffs another"~~
"load"  "sold" – sold him – got a load on them
gag
dodge — ("that was only a dodge")
such words as
              Hurry–graphs, (the name of a book of sketches)

___

(?) chapparral

___

    peon

___

    doctrinaire     (
          lay–brother – theorist.
(doctorate)
soi (self)
        soi disant     self–stylist     would–be

seance   (see ā́nz)   n. f.
pl   seances)   sitting — a meeting   seaten  [ ? ]
              (the spiritualists held a seance)

[30: blank]

[31: green sheet:]
pantaloons – "pants" – trowsers (what root?)
——breeches—

Do not these words illustrate a law of language, namely, that with the introduction of any new thing, (as the pantaloons) the word, from the same land or source, is introduced with them?

Family names
  Surnames —
Roman style of names — Greek
American aborigines
Japan — India — Peninsulas
   Sumatra Borneo

Russian — American aborigin[es]

[32: green sheet:]
   Yes, I think these now Nursery Tales, were originally in the infancy of literature of epics, and of mental amusements, told as relaxing tales to great warriors, kings, and heroes — and had good nutriment for them too.

[33: Williamsburgh tax form, clipped:]
  All The fables, now for children, Jack and his Bean–Pole, the (two more) Beauty and the Beast, Tom Thumb and the fables that animals talk, are doubtless modern editions of the tales told, recited, perhaps sung, ages and ages ago, to our full-grown Scandinavian, or Kymry Teutonic, or Brit or Gallic, or Italian ancestors or ancestresses, heroes, warriors, youths, and women. —

[34: blank]

[35: green sheet:]     A. U. C.
  Scantlings      Year from the building of
            the City of Rome

fiasco
> (he suffered fiasco)

---

[Clipping:] 👉

ANCIENT NURSERY TALES. — Tom Thumb first appears in English legendary lore, in print, in the year 1630. He is supposed, however, to be of Anglo-Saxon lineage. The stories of "Jack in the Bean Stalk," "Puss in Boots," "Jack the Giant Killer," "Beauty and the Beast," etc., are all from the North, and are still to be found in the nursery [?] of Scandinavia.

---

Not only these quaint little tales, but many words, trace back in the same manner, of course.

At first these stories were poems, romances, no doubt for grown person[s], even kings, gatherings, festivities, warriors. — Then they subsided by degrees to be told to children, as many of what is now among men will subside. —

[36: blank]

[37: pale yellow sheet:]
Flanges of Words
> (namely, those rims that come out on the main words)

~~on~~ the flange is the variation, or rim, considered separately from the main word.

---

rune ⎫
runic ⎭

Language characters of the Goths, Scandinavians, &c

---

Poems, traditions of the ancient northern Europeans

---

"cut loose"   (railroad men's term
> Fred's explanation).

---

indigene   (indigenous)

—

(as cotton is an indigene of ~~parts of~~ Africa and Asia

[38: blank]

[39: pale yellow sheet:]
> (an axiom about language

---

Talk to everybody    everywhere — try it on — keep it up — <u>real</u> talk — no
   airs — real questions — no one will be offended — or    if any one is,
   that will teach the offender just as any one else

[Clipping:]

KING JAMES' BIBLE. — For many years before the death of Queen Elizabeth,
the question of a revised translation of the Scriptures had been frequently
agitated. Upon the ascension of James the subject was pressed with new ardor,
and the consent of the monarch was at last obtained to favor the project. Taking the matter into his own hands, he soon completed the requisite arrangements, which were on a scale surpassing all that had been witnessed in England in the way of Bible translation. Before the close of July, 1604, fifty-four
scholars had been selected as translators, and divided into six companies, two
of which were to meet at Westminster, and two at each of the universities.
Ample provision was made from the royal treasury for the maintenance and
remuneration of the translators. After great care in its preparation, the version
was published in 1614, with a dedication to the king, in which flattery was
carried to its culminating point. The work was not immediately received
with the unanimity for which James had hoped. Attempts were made to
supersede it by a new translation in 1652, and in 1656, but were unsuccessful.

[40: blank]

[41: white lined sheet, clipped:]
        Virginia idioms
   — "How's all"?
   —

   "Where you been at?"

[42: blank]

[43: pale yellow sheet:]
<u>a good innovation</u>

      employer   —   employee
      offender    —   offendee
                          thing offended
                              d
      server     —  servee
      lover      — ⎰ lovee
                   ⎱ thing loved
      hater      — ⎰ hatee
                   ⎰ thing hated

suspecter  —  suspectee
receiver  —  ? ~~receivee~~
        ? receiver
        ? (thing received

[44: blank]

[45: pale yellow sheet:]
[ danseuse (n. f.) dãn swũeez
  debut

[Clipping:]

At the conclusion of the address, Dr. D. Francis Bacon came forward and delighted the audience for another hour. The subject was one of peculiar local interest, it being an essay on the great number of languages spoken daily in the city of New York, the classification amounting to no less *than eighty different languages* (not dialects,) in constant use in this city. The learned Doctor spoke ex-tempore, and interspersed his remarks with an occasional digression and anecdote, highly acceptable to his hearers. No city in the world can furnish a parallel to this in the number of its spoken languages. Dr. Bacon has expended much labor and research on the subject of his remarks before the Society, and his varied illustrations evinced great power and ability. The Doctor has evidently been "round some," and in the course of his remarks he stated that at a week's notice he could place before the Society persons of both sexes, resident here, who spoke *sixty different languages,* and that they should converse with each other in their mother tongues!

The remaining twenty, to make up the whole number spoken, he could get, with a little more time and trouble!

It is to be hoped that this interesting communication will be placed before the public shortly.

Before the adjournment, it was announced that the Society have recently had placed at their disposal, (temporarily,) by different members, and individuals, several fine original paintings, illustrating French history, and which we learned were to furnish the basis for two or three lectures at the Society's fine rooms. The first will be given on *Thursday evening next, 11th inst.*

N. Y. Hist. Society
? (or Geograph. Soc) 1857–8

---

Roster – a plan or table by which the duties of military officers are marked
    out. —

[46: blank]

[47: green sheet:]
Evangel — good–news
well–hung — This phase, applied to a man — organically of Has organic
good principals, not disposed to meanness or dirty dirtiness.— Bodily,
possessed of his full share of the manly ability xx with women. —

passe–passe (päs päs pä-s pá-s
trick — slight of hand

[48: blank]

[49: green sheet:]
Words out of places or persons as
Bayonet – from Bayonne, in France
Daguerreotype, from Daguerre

[Clipping:]

PARTS OF SPEECH. — It is asserted that in the English language proper, apart
from technical and scientific terms, there are 20,500 nouns, 40 pronouns, 9,200
adjectives, 8,000 verbs, 2,600 adverbs, 60 prepositions, 19 conjuctions, 68 inter-
jections, and two articles. Acording to Webster's Dictionary, there are one
hundred thousand words in the language.

? certify this first

[Clipping:]

A.R. – Badinage is pronouned bad-e-*nazh;* mirage, mi-*razh;* protege, pro-
ta-*zah;* rouge, *roozh,* etc. In these words the *g* has the sound of *zh.*
protege  pró–ta=zhā

bizarre  )   (odd, queer,)

[50: blank]

[51: green sheet:]
see Addison on English Language
——————    in German "British Authors"
Words of Epitaphs

Kanyon (cañon,] a Spanish word, a barrel, tube, piece of artillery (passage

of a river between high sides)
Kiooshk (a no pleasant roofed apartment in a garden, with flowers, seats, and
    sometimes a fountain

---

vis inertia (the power or stamina of inertness)
  vis viva (–force of motion — the power or staminat of active life)
(terms of physical science)

[52: blank]

[53: green sheet:]
                          lustrum (five years) ancient Rome

Johnson's Dictionary
    First pub. 1755    (was this <u>first</u> good dictionary of English?)
                           (O no)

---

orthography
etymology – origin of words – parts of speech, in grammar
syntax — constructing sentences
prosody – accent, metre, rhyme & rythm   smoothness &c. both in prose and
    verse

---

[On a small scrap pasted in:]
Zazzia (Italian  a foray – a sudden rush and seizure

Capponiere   kap–pon–néer  French  (fortification   a passage, protected
    each side, leading from one part of the works to another

[54: blank]

[55: green sheet:]
ē ti ŏl ō gy – (an account of the causes of any thing, particular[l]y diseases)

---

about the controversy respecting words ending in <u>ick</u> – the k left out by modern writers — If any thing is left out it were better the c — thus musik, stik,
lok, brik, apoplektik —

These little controversies are miserable, ~~things~~ in such a great thing as lan-
    guage

---

kidnapt

worshipt
gallopt
developt

[56: blank]

[57: green sheet:]
        –~~get H~~

"Although neither the origin nor subsequent progress of English can be assigned to any specific dates, yet, for the sake of perspicuity we may, – (as in the case of general history,) establish arbitrary and conventional divisions. — Thus we say, generally speaking, that about 1150 may be dated the decline of pure Saxon; about 1250 the commencement of English; and that the century between these two dates was occupied by a sort of semi–Saxon language."

                         Hippisley, a late English writer. —

1066   William the Conqueror
      —

      Then the Norman French became the language of the courts and
          upper classes
      Still Anglo–Saxon continued to be spoken by the old inhabitants and
          the common people.
      But the laws, judgments, pleadings &c were in Norman French till
1362   Edward 3ᵈ by statute enacted ~~th~~ English as the language for s<u>peaking</u>
      law proceedings, but French for writing them.

[58: blank]

[59: green sheet:]
(100,000 words are said to be now in the repertoire) ?is not the no. greater
      than 38,000 – yet the whole no must be twice that
"The English Language consists of about 38000 words. — This includes of
      course, not only radical words, but all derivatives, except the preterits
      and participles of verbs — of these (38 000) about <u>23,000</u> or nearly
      five–eighths are of Anglo–Saxon origin"
                         Edinburgh Review vol 70
Probably Perhaps <u>now</u> the plentiful contributions of foreign words have made
  ?   the proportion to stand half and half. —

     ~~Perhaps there are~~

[60: blank]

[61: green sheet:]

Charleston Book 1846

Greek

eulogistic:

[Clipping:]

Mr. Legaré, as is known, was widely read in classic literature — and had, in particular, an unbounded admiration for the Greek genius. In this admiration we are disposed to join him so fully, that we cannot refrain from quoting, out of the volume before us, an eloquent eulogium on the Greek language.

It is impossible to contemplate the annals of Greek literature and art, without being struck with them, as by far the most extraordinary and brilliant phenomenon in the history of the human mind. The very language, even in its primitive simplicity, as it came down from the rhapsodists who celebrated the exploits of Hercules and Theseus, was as great a wonder as any it records. All the other tongues that civilized men have spoken, are poor, and feeble, and barbarous, in comparison with it. Its compass and flexibility, its riches and its powers, are altogether unlimited. It not only expresses with precision all that is thought or known at any given period, but it enlarges itself naturally with the progress of science, and affords, as if without an effort, a new phrase, or a systematic nomenclature whenever one is called for. It is equally adapted to every variety of style and subject — to the most shadowy subtlety of distinction, and the utmost exactness of definition, as well as to the energy and pathos of popular eloquence — to the majesty, the elevation, the variety of the Epic, and the boldest license of the Dithyrambic, no less than to the sweetness of the Elegy, the simplicity of the Pastoral, or the heedless gayety and delicate characterization of Comedy. Above all, what is an unspeakable charm — a sort of *naiveté* is peculiar to it, and appears in all these various styles, and is quite as becoming and agreeable in an historian or a philosopher — Xenephon, for instance — as in the light and jocund numbers of Anacreon. Indeed, were there no other object in the learning Greek, but to see to what perfection language is capable of being carried, not only as a medium of communication, but as an instrument of thought, we see not why the time of a young man would not be just as well bestowed in acquiring a knowledge of it — for all the purposes, at least, of a liberal or elementary education — as in learning Algebra, another specimen of a language or arrangement of signs, perfect in its kind. But this wonderful idiom happens to have been spoken, as was hinted in the preceding paragraph, by a race as wonderful. The very first monument of their genius, the most ancient relic of letters in the Western world, stands to this day altogether unrivalled in the exalted class to which it belongs. What was the history of this immortal poem, and of its great fellow?

Was it a single individual, and who was he, that composed them? Had he any master or model? What had been his education, and what was the state of society in which he lived? These questions are full of interest to a philosophic inquirer into the intellectual history of the species, but they are especially important with a view to the subject of the present discussion. Whatever causes for the matchless excellence of these primitive poems, and for that of the language in which they are written, will go far to explain the extraordinary circumstance, that the same favored people left nothing unattempted in philosophy, in letters, and in arts, and attempted nothing without signal, and, in some cases, unrivalled success.

[62: blank]

[63: small white scrap:]
fusillade
~~while this fusillade was going on~~ – several shots were fired in the cloisters
– crowds, attracted by the noise of the fusillade, swarmed round the windows)
battue
  (they formed a circle round the gardens and large grounds and forced the priests by blows, to enter the church – While this battue was going on outside

[64: lines of poetry, sideways:]
                    the
Here ~~there~~ are the    lands that
        ~~at last – they~~
    equalities
Here ~~and the~~ ~~politics, th~~
        ~~women, men, civili~~
            rights equalities, civiliz
    ~~proofs;~~
        so far the
        ~~final~~ ~~last~~ only
    ~~and last~~ descendant
    ~~the time – the~~ of all
    and growths of the ~~earth~~
Here at last advances the soul
    durable ~~and final~~ fruit of all things – the

[65: clipped from Williamsburgh tax form:]
"Ultra–marine" }     ~~at~~ beyond the seas,
             }         also blue

a term to be applied to ~~all ls~~ foreign–spirited literats as opposed to those who compose their works with sole regard to the American spirit and facts.

[66: blank]

[67: clipped from Williamsburgh tax form:]
The word wanted for the male and female act
        "clinch"

[68: blank]

[69: green sheet:]
    Words of the Bible
        Bible Literature
    What powerful and quite indefinable words have been contributed by the proper nouns of the Old Testament — the names of the Deity — of Hell, of Heaven — of the great persons —

Words of figures — or rather the figures themselves
— for
Figures are words
        every number ~~an~~ or calculation in numbers is a poem

[70: blank]

[71: green sheet:]
Epithets of hatred, anger, sorrow, &c

villain, (old meaning, merely an inferior person)
scoundrel
damn!
Wo!

Epithets of endearment,
love – beloved —
My dear

[72: blank]

[73: green sheet:]
    changes in the meaning of words
        The word "demon"

Socrates had his demon –
   the word, ~~in its ancient~~ till toward modern times, having ~~only~~ as much
   the signification of spirit, or one of the genii, or heavenly visitor, as of an
   evil spirit. —

   Prononcé /     strongly marked – or prominent

[74: blank]

[75: pale yellow sheet:]
lunatic — ("looney")
————————

imam — (preacher)
Kaliph — (successor)
sierra – a saw (~~sa~~ as a carpenter's saw with teeth)
puerto — a gate – a "port"
cordillera – mountain range composed of many small parallel ranges — (as a
   cord is formed of several strands twisted together)
————————————————————————————————————————————

"spoor"   ~~track~~ signs, track, or trail ~~or the~~ of an animal &c. followed by
   hunters in Africa or Australia — viz: all the signs, footprints, ~~track~~
   broken limbs, dung, moisture, or any other indications

[76: blank]

[77: pale yellow sheet:]
   <u>political, electioneering, party words</u> —
loco focos
black republicans
abolitionists
free soilers
know–nothings
? whigs, (what a ridiculous name for an American party
tories ——————
"posted up" — (a most expressive phrase, derived from account–keeping)
loot
boodle

[78: blank]

[79: pale yellow sheet:]
absences — ("his mind was full of absences.")

apostle     (literally <u>one sent by</u> <u>another</u>

[80: blank]

[81: green sheet:]
doctrinaire — theorist

[Clipping:]

NAMES. — Names have mnemonic power; a vocabulary of their meanings would be as sweet as the songs of the Troubadors. It would be like breaking into old royal tombs, the laying bare of old battle fields, the disclosing of old fossils. We should wonder how much of poetry, of history, of biography, may be wrapped up in a couple of syllables; what pictures may be painted with a word or two. The learned language of Europe can have nothing more beautiful than the dialects of the red children of the West; and yet that word "dilapidated" — it would take the happiest day that Angelo ever saw to paint it; the stone apart from stone, the crumbling wall, the broken turret strewn among the weeds. That word "disaster'd" — without a star; so pity him, the poet sings: "in his own loose revolving field, the swain disaster'd stands." What a night, what a *winter's* night was that! The history of a race may be folded in a word. The "curfew" that tolls in Gray's Elegy — what a tale its tones are telling of the times of the old Norman; how it lets us into the secret of domestic economy eight centuries ago: how it sets the bells a ringing, and covers the Saxon fires, and plays Othello with the light of home.

— *Chicago Journal.*

[Clipping:]

If it be a sign of richness in a language that a single word is used to express many quite different things, the good old English may be regarded as the Rothschild of languages. For instance, how many significations lie in that single monosyllable *box?* It means, a stall in a stable, a solitary table in a tavern, a private place in a theater, a snuff-magazine in a pocket, a slap in the face, a certain tree in a garden, the nave in a wheel, the compass in a ship, the throne of the coachman, a chest, a goblet, a dose of pills, without even reckoning the manifold acceptations which children, ladies, printers and mechanics of every kind have given to the word. *Sport* is another of these multifarious expressions. It is indifferently applied to a horse-race, a steeplechase, a cricket-match, a regatta, a yacht trip, a rowing club, a boat-race, a pedestrian performance, a boxing match, gymnastics, cock and rat fighting, dog baiting, a mat of rush, the pleasure of teasing, etc. Whatever gives exercise to the body without calling in the mind is expressed by this favorite and truly British word; and nothing could afford [a] better insight into English manners and propensities than the multiple meanings of this assemblage of five letters. We can thus, at one glance, see that the three great requisites of English life are

"The chase, the race, the liberty to roam."

[82: blank]

[83: green sheet:]
    Name for lectures
                Lessons En Passant
    Lessons – No. 2 – No. 7, &c &c
    (as "Walt Whitman's Lessons")

---

(savoir (sa voar) v. a.
      to know
      to be aware of –"posted up"
  "    v. n. to be learned – a scholar
(savoir-vivre (n. m.) to have sa-voar – vi-vr (fine manners — either for a
   gentleman or lady
savoir faire
     — expert – skill – wits  ———

---

Bouleversement — upset – overthrow – confusion

---

Boulevard    }    rampart – security
Boulevard    }    — wall
                seems to be a pleasure–walk, ground, with trees, as outside
    the thicker demesnes of a town. —

[84: blank]

[85: white scrap of paper:]
—————— kil-k: sho's
quelque–chose (anything)

---

mes soeurs (mysisters)
? (Bon camerado)

---

Cōnfrère
      kon-frȧre
      (brother, co–worker, intimate associate, &c, as of the same religious
      order, trade, or place.)

[86: printed matter, a poem (or advertisement) about Pfaff's — 12 lines from a much longer piece]

[87: green sheet:]                                    or
Idiópathy (gr.) — peculiar affection or feeling – A primary disease or a disease
    ~~not~~ belonging to the part affected — not arising from sympathy with
    other parts

---

Monolith, an obolisk or monument (one) — a single stone.

[88: blank]

[89: four slips of Williamsburgh blue tax forms:]
Attempts, &c.
        for words
Opera – ~~(its~~ in the sense of work, labor, or the action of the processes or
    product of labor)
"&c." — Why not use the term "&c." in my poems?
masc. } orator
fem.  } oratress  } oratist    both masc & fem.
m        reader
fem.    readress } readist — both m & f

[90: blank]

[91: blank]

[92: blank]

[93: four different kinds of white scraps pasted to a green sheet:]
    fornication

---

The Bib. meaning of this word is said to be <u>idolatry</u>
        (whoredom in Bib. often means idolatry.)
?    Fuimus — Fuimus
        Words

---

"Romance language" or languages    see Ellis's book pp. 1, 2, &c

[94: blank]

[95: green sheet:]

[Clipping:]

One of the larger articles is on the interesting subject of "Americanisms." It is mentioned in the course of it that "two vocabularies of Americanisms have been published, one at Boston, by John Pickering, in 1816, and the other at New York, by John Russell Bartlett, in 1848." It might have been added that an abridged translation of Bartlett's book has appeared in Dutch — a singular fact — and that there is a dictionary of English and German, by Elwell, published at New York in 1850, in which many Americanisms are included and pointed out by a distinguishing mark. To put this distinguishing mark, and put it rightly, seems to be a task transcending the powers of any individual, and we would recommend the Philological Society, when they have sufficient leisure from the labors of their new gigantic dictionary, to appoint a mixed commission of English and Yankees to endeavor, if possible, to draw the boundary line to the satisfaction of both nations. The best way to begin would, perhaps, be to take a popular American novel, and have a discussion on each word or phrase that sounded strange to an English ear. It would probably be found that many of them were equally strange to natives of different portions of the United States; and, on the other hand, it would certainly be found that many phrases which Americans would set down as Americanisms were as English as Addison. In the article on Americanisms in the Cyclopaedia it is amusing to see what odd misconceptions on that score occur. "Politician," we are told, "in the United States, means a person who busies himself with the management and contests of a political party. In England it means a statesman." In England there is a tolerably famous painting, known by the name of "The Village Politicians," which shows that the term is not so stately a character. Again, "Stage is the American term for a stage-coach, and it is sometimes, but rarely, used in that sense by the English." "Stage is certainly now used but rarely in that sense, because stages are themselves a rarity, but the word only disappeared with the thing. Further, we are told that "Ride, in the United States, means riding either in a wagon or on horseback. The English restrict "ride" to horseback. . . . Ride was formerly used by the English as it is now used by the Americans." One would like extremely to know when English people ceased to "ride in a coach," and what is the word that has displaced it. But the richest piece of information for the English reader is that contained in the notice of the word "ticket" —

"Ticket is used by the Americans in many ways unknown to the English. When an American engages a passage on a railroad he purchases a ticket — the Englishman is booked at the box office. The American purchases a "through ticket" or a "way ticket" — the Englishman is booked for a portion or the whole distance of the intended journey."

If the writer of "Americanisms" should ever take a journey to England, which he evidently has not done hitherto, he will find that his "Americanisms," "way ticket" excepted, are the current language of every railway station in or out of Cockneydom.

alto-relievo (alto relief)
———— figures very boldly standing out from the background, but not altogether ~~stan~~ out)

———————————————

    among idiomatic ~~terms~~ forms "&c."     (how can this be translated?)

[Another clipping:]

INDIAN NAMES — 'Poor,' or 'pore,' which is found to make the termination of so many Indian cities and settlements, signifies town. Thus Nagpore means the town of serpents — a definition, by the way, sufficiently appropriate when we reflect on the treacherous character of the Sepoys by whom it was so recently garrisoned. 'Abad' and 'patam' also signify town; Hyderabad being Hyder's Town, and Seringapatam — from Seringa, a name of a god Vishnu — being the town of Seringa. Allahabad, from 'Allah,' God, and 'abad' abode, means the abode of God, that city being the capital of Agra, the chief school of the Brahmins, and much restorted to by pilgrims.' Punjab is the country of the Five Rivers, and Doab is applied to a part of a country between two rivers.

[96: blank]

[97: scrap of white paper:]
    Words
    ————

    35–6 &c
see pp ~~37–8~~     ~~&c~~     "Hebrew Politics"

[98: blank]

[99: green sheet:]
(good term)
    passe    n. m. pä sā    au passe    (in the past)
              ō pä sā

[Clipping:]

    Sir John Bowring — the late Chinese Governor o[f] England, and lately lecturing on China in the city of Glasgow — has asserted that the lexicon of the Chinese language consists of seventy volumes. M. Stanislaus Julien, Professor of Chinese at the College de France, and the first Sinologist in Europe, has written to the *Constitutionnel* to point out Sir John's mistake. M. Julien states that in reality, the imperial dictionary of the Emperor TShanghi — being that which all European students of Chinese use — is only thirty-two volumes in 12mo., not thicker than the little finger, and containing only 42,713 characters. M. Julien asserts, moreover, that a knowledge of about one tenth of these characters is sufficient to enable Chinese books to be understood, and that the Chinese language "is as clear as the easiest of modern languages" — the proof being, he says, that numerous Chinese works have been translated into the French in the course of the last thirty years.

[100: blank]

[101: green sheet:]
exploité    pap
exploiter — to cultivate or make the most of (–for sale)
(orig)
exploitee (one cultivating and making use of – working – part owner)

[102: blank]

[103: white sheet:]
            Words
Effective – [Fr] [com]3437 p. 429, Wb. Dict.    specie or coin as dist. from paper money[.] Thus a draft may be stipulated to be paid in effective, as dist.c't from greenbacks, or any depr.    a military term    a pap. writer in Ed. Review, Oct. 1870, speaks of "the peace effective of the cavalry"

Ei-do-lon    (Gr)
    phantom – the image of an Helen, at Troy instead of a real flesh & blood woman

[104: blank, lined page]

[105: blank, green sheet]

[106: blank]

3437.  These square brackets occur in the MS.

[107: small scrap of buff paper:]
The <u>Girls l'Amour</u>    love-girls

[108: blank]

[109: green sheet:]
    The learning of the Spartan youth was very narrow, according to what would be our modern estimate; but they were taught to express themselves with purity and conciseness: hence the term <u>laconic</u>, from Laconia, the province in which Sparta was situated —

[110: blank]

[111: three different kinds of white scraps pasted to a green sheet:]
<u>Mythras</u>, in old Persian mysteries, was the name of the sun
<u>Mylitta</u>, that of the moon
                      (the earth)
(rondure)    "this huge <u>rondure</u> on which we rest."
    Gilsons – Beans     Cor. Sudbry & Court   adv. of a hog hitched to a carriage

[112: blank, both on the back of the white scraps and the green sheet, both sides]

[113: two different white scraps pasted to a green sheet:]
literatus  ~~he~~ Casletar says of D'Israeli, "he was a great <u>literatus</u>"
    <u>Phrases – Expressions – &c</u>
<u>Mobile</u> – as applied to the face &c. full of changing expression – very ductile

[114: blank, both scraps]

[115: green sheet:]
[Clipping:]
    To be able to speak many languages, as the voluble French, the courtly Italian, the lofty Spanish, the lusty Dutch, the powerful Latin, the scientific and happily-compounding Greek, the most spacious Slavonique, the mystical Hebrew with all her dialects — all this is but vanity and superficial knowledge, unless the inward man be bettered hereby; unless by seeing and perusing

the volume of the great world one learn to know the little, which is himself; unless one learn to govern and check the passions, our domestic enemies, than which nothing can conduce more to gentleness of mind, to elegancy of manners, and solid wisdom. But principally, unless by surveying and admiring his works abroad, one improve himself in the knowledge of his Creator, *præ quo quisquilliæ cætera;* in comparison whereof the best sublunary blessings are but baubles, and this indeed, this *unum necessarium* should be the end to which travel should tend. — *James Howell, 1642.*

[116: blank]

[117: salmon sheet:]
impropriety of the word "petition" as used for memorials to Congress, Legislatures, Common Councils &c. — It sprung up under the very state of society which America has arisen to destroy, and only belongs there.

[118: blank:]

[119: green sheet:]
sans souci
diablerie

[Clipping:]

Language. — Sir John Bowring, at a recent Tract Society meeting, said: — "The Chinese are a proud nation, and naturally enough. Their language has existed for four thousand and five hundred years, and everybody reads it. Our language is a language of yesterday. A person who lived in the island of Great Britain eight hundred years ago, could not understand one of us, and we could not make ourselves understood by him. But Confucius wrote six and seven hundred years before Jesus Christ, and his language is read not by fifty or sixty millions, who understand the English language, but, by five hundred millions of the human race.

[120: blank]

[121: salmon sheet:]
conclusion vol. 1 / Max Müller (in Bunsens work)
If now we gaze from our native shores over that vast ocean of human speech, with its waves rolling on from continent to continent, rising under the fresh breezes of the morning of history, and slowly heaving in our own more sultry atmosphere — with sails gliding over its surface, and many an oar ploughing through its surf, and the flags of all nations waving joyously together — with its rocks and wrecks, its storms and battles, yet reflecting

serenely all that is beneath and above and around it — If we gaze and hearken
to the strange sounds rushing past our ears in unbroken strains, it seems no
longer a wild tumult or                    but we feel as if placed within
some ancient cathedral, listening to innumerable voices; — and the more
intensely we listen, the more all discords melt away into higher harmonies,
till at last we hear but one majestic trichord, or a mighty unison, as at the
end of a sacred harmony.

[122: blank]

[123: smaller salmon sheet:]
    Such visions will float through the str [?] of the grammarian, and in
the midst of toil[some] researches his heart will suddenly beat, as he f[eels]
the conviction growing upon him that men are brethren in the simplest sense
of the word — the children of the same Father — whatever their country,
their color, thir language, or their faith. —

[124: blank]

[125: blue Williamsburgh tax form:]
    In Italy, and all countries of Roman origin, or previously ~~included~~ remain-
ing any ~~length~~ long time in their empire, the Latin language remained a
living tongue, much spoken, and more than all others written, until the ninth
or tenth century. —

[126: blank]

[127: green sheet:]
entourage (azh) (a as in man — railing (round a theatre) mounting (of
    gems)      persons around

---

    ~~da~~  dancing    soiree

---

padre

senora

---

goitre
crevasse
matrix

---

gossoon (a youth more than child and less than man)

[128: blank]

[129: white scrap:]
quien sabe   kēēn śa – ve ("who knows")
Deōs   sabe ("God knows")

[130:]
No 9, goes up by Treas. 10:25     down – 11:10

[131: green sheet:]
    Names of Persons —

These are very curious to trace out. — ~~Whence~~ How came they? Whence
    these Marys, Johns, Williams, and Elizabeths? —

shin–dig
spree
bender
bummer

[132: blank]

[133: white scrap, lined on both sides:]
    April
from from the Latin verb     Aperio – "I open" (April was anciently $2^d$ month
    of year)

[134: blank]

[135: green sheet:]
    happifying

a phrase of the race–course of a horse
    "he's got the foot" or "he hasn't got the foot to do it"

[Clipping:]

### SOMETHING ABOUT SURNAMES.

The names of persons offer curious etymologies. Of course, the trades of
the hunter, fisher, archer (*arc,* a bow), fletcher (*fleche,* an arrow), smith,
glover, etc., have given us many surnames. Grosvenor (*gros veneur*) was chief
huntsman to the Norman dukes. All the Reads, Reeds, Reids were originally

*red* men. Bunker was so named from his good heart (*bon cœur*). But few have observed that old Dan Chaucer had a French shoemaker in his ancestry (*chausser*), and the Spenser was by lineage a *butler,* whose place was in the spense or buttery; nor need he be ashamed, for his company is that of the Lords Despencer. Perhaps it was the danger of such a category that caused the haughty sovereigns of Spain to have no name for public use beyond the purlieus of royalty. They only sign themselves *Yo el Rey* and *Yo la Reina.* — *Lippincott's Magazine.*

[136: blank]

[137: green sheet:]
   cannaille — ("doggery")
gobe–mouches        pl flycatcher     idler – trifler of no opinion
go-be-mou-sh
[Clipping from a book:]

---

SECT. CLIII. — EPITHETS.

1   THE meaning of the word *Wretch* is one not generally understood. It
2 was originally, and is now, in some parts of England, used as a term of the
    softest and fondest tenderness. This is not the only instance in which words
3 in their present general acceptation bear a very opposite meaning to what
    they did in former times. The word *Wench,* formerly, was not used in the
4 low and vulgar acceptation that it is at present. *Damsel* was the appellation
    of young ladies of quality, and *Dame* a title of distinction. *Knave* once signi-
5 fied a servant; and in an early translation of the New Testament, instead
6 of "Paul the Servant," we read "Paul the Knave of Jesus Christ."
    DEFINITIONS, &c. — *Epithet* — a name applied to a person or thing. Define *tenderness, instance, originally, acceptation, opposite, appellation, ladies of quality,* (ladies of the highest rank,) *signified, translation.*

---

chamade    Fr (sha – mãd)     the beat of the drum, as a signal for parley
        or surrender

---

coiffe (koa-f) head dress
coiffeur    (koa fure)    man head dresser
coiffeuse            woman    "    "

[138: blank]

[139: green sheet:]

Spoor (the track or trail of animals – (in Africa) (why not in America or anywhere?)

roturier     (plebeian)

coupee

canard     (duck)

---

earl – (title of honor) – Earl seems to come from a word meaning <u>strength</u>

[Clipping:]

— B. B. "Cicisbeo" is an Italian term applied to a lady-dangler, but with an augmentation of meaning not wholly, perhaps, Italian, though less fully implied by the English word.

good ⎰ renaissance (n.f.) second birth   regeneration   re–sprouting up

           rĕ    nà    sān – s

      ⎱ renaissant (adj) spring up again

---

good ⎛ rencontre     (n.f.)

[140: blank]

[141: green sheet: blank]

[142: blank]

[143: green sheet:]

Words arising out of the geography, agriculture, and natural traits of a country — such as many of the Southern words — also Eastern and Western words — Many idiomatic phrases

In the South, words that have sprouted up from the dialect and peculiarities of the slaves. — the Negroes. — The south is full of negro–words. — Their idioms and pronunciation are heard every where

[144: blank]

[145: green sheet:]

[Clipping:]

### Names.

The inappropriateness of many of the names under which the human race is compelled to pass through the world becomes ridiculously apparent upon carefully examining a directory of any large city. In our own we find that we have a population which are included in this misfortune. Females, according to the proper significance of their family names, are Bakers, Fishers, Hackmen, Hunters, Oatmen, Pollmen, Smiths, Wrights, Gardners, Melters, Millers, Pipers, Spearmen, Turners, Wagners, and extensive Walkers; beside which trades those of Cook, Cutter, Dyer, Sower, Spicer, Tailor, Wheeler, and many others are represented in the list. We also find feminine Kings, Lords, Sages, Mayors, Sargeants, Drakes, and Swains, and large numbers bearing the masculine names of Thomas, Daniel, Henry, Jackson, John, Lucas, Oliver, Paul, Philip, &c., while male bipeds are designated as Queen, Belle, Rose, Duck, and other female names. Then we have the suggestive names White, Green, Brown, Black, Grey, Dun, Hope, Love, Neighbor, Savage, Brooks, Bone, Cable, Gale, Hopper, Sunrise, Ward, Boil, Death, Ford, Cash, Heart, Home, Hull, Reason, Will, Hood, Hall, Love, Palm, Price, Sterling, and Well, representing both sexes. In the way of animals, birds, &c., may be found Wolf, Fox, Beaver, Crow, Robin, Coon, Martin, and Shrimps. Merchandise and manufactures are represented by Bees, Steel, Stone, Wood, Brandy, Rice, Ham, Hood, and Wheat. Time is designated by May, Day, Week, Winter, &c. The nations by French, Holland, Welsh, German, and English. Distance by Long, Short, Mile, and Foot. Quality by Gross, Peck, Gill, and Speck. Physical organization by Cheek, Stout, Strong, Short, Leg, Foot, Hand, Heart, Blood.

[Another clipping:]

## Provincialisms.

"Doless" must be of Pennsylvania German origin though we cannot track it. The same is true of "donsey." "Or'nary" is "ordinary," cut down, and is one of the commonest provincialisms. "Right-smart" generally qualifies a noun. Only in speaking of health, we believe, is right smart used as an adverb. We know that "rock" is generally used for stone in the Southwest; but "whet-rock" we have never heard. Poke is in common use in the South, and is good old Chaucerian English, and still lives in England in the proverbial phrase from Chaucer, "A pig in a poke." "There once lived near the Alleghanies 'ornary' people (and things). Many in 'dog-days' were 'donsey-like' (languid or sick). The words mighty, right-smart, heap, etc., have a varied meaning in parts of the West, determined more by custom than fitness. 'That's a mighty-peart baby.' 'Wife is right-smart worse. She's had a heap o' chills; tuk a power o' doctor stuff, an' got down mighty weak an' poar.' 'Is ther ayery letter for we uns?' 'Can you uns help tote logs in the new ground? there's nary day to spare if we clar it in time for a crap.' 'Here, Jimmy, roll this rock till I grind my mowing-blade; and you, Johnny, get the whet-rock and a poke (little-bag) of apples, and put them on the slide (a little sled). Custom sanctions 'right-smart chance o' people, heap o' wind and rain, heap o' sand.' The jovial driver tells his jolly passengers to 'pile in.' 'Grub pile' is the welcome call to meals for Western river boatmen. The horsemen is asked to 'alight,' and his 'nag' is watered at the 'branch.' "

In Virginia a horseman speaks of carrying his horse when he is travelling; in other sections of the country the horse is supposed to carry the man. In estimating distance, "right-smart" is the phrase invariably applied, whether the miles be one or a dozen.

[146: blank]

[147: green sheet:]
  Words to be re–instated

---

Door-(Teutonic) to deafen or stupefy with noise)
[White lined scrap with notation:]
      Wash. Chronicle     Jan 31, 1870

[Clipping glued to white scrap:]

#### CHANGES IN NAMES OF VESSELS.

As quite a number of conflicting newspaper statements have been made at times concerning the change of names of United States vessels, the following, transmitted from the Secretary of the Navy to the House of Representatives, will give the only correct information on that subject:

NAVY DEPARTMENT
WASHINGTON, January 22, 1870.

SIR: In compliance with the resolution of the House of Representatives passed on the 13th inst., I have the honor to submit herewith a list of the vessels of the United States navy, the names of which have been changed since the 4th of March, 1869.

The changes in the names of the vessels have been made to conform with the resolution of March 3, 1819, (Statutes at Large, vol. 3, page 538,) and the act of June 12, 1858, (Statutes at Large, vol. 11, page 319,) which require vessels of the first class to be named after States, those of the second and third classes after rivers, cities, or towns, and others by the Secretary of the Navy, as the President may direct.

I am, respectfully, your obedient servant,
GEO. M. ROBESON,
Secretary of the Navy.
Hon. JAMES G. BLAINE,
Speaker of the House of Representatives.

*First Class Vessels — Changed to Names of States.*

  Neshaminy to Nevada.
  Ammonoosuc to Iowa.

  Kewaydin to Pen[n]sylvania
  Madawaska to Tennessee.
  Minnetonka to California.
  Ontario to New York.
  Piscataqua to Delaware.
  Pompanoosuc to Connecticut.
  Passaconaway to Massachusetts.
  Quinsigamond to Oregon.
  Shakamaxon to Nebraska.
  Wampanoag to Florida.

*Second and Third Class Changed to Names of Rivers, Cities, or Towns.*

  Mosholu to Severn.
  Pushmataha to Congress.
  Algoma to Bencia.
  Contoocook to Albany.
  Kenosha to Plymouth.
  Manitou to Worcester.

*Iron-Clad Vessels, Less Than Third-Class, Named by the President's Direction.*

  Casco to Hero.
  Chimo to Piscataqua.
  Kalamazoo to Colossus.
  Kickapoo to Kewaydin.
  Manayunk to Ajax.
  Naubuc to Minnetonka.
  Neosho to Osceolo.
  Sangamon to Jason.
  Shiloh to Iris.
  Squando to Algoma.
  Tippacanoe to Wyandotte.
  Tunxis to Otsego.
  Waxsaw to Niobe.
  Tonawanda to Amphitrite.
  Agamenticus to Terror.

  Of this latter class eleven have been in commission, and Congress has authorized their sale as unfit for service.

[148: blank]

[149: white unevenly cut scrap:]

"Nicknames" said Napoleon, "are not to be despised — for it is v̶e̶r̶y̶ largely by such names, people are swayed & governed"

[150: at edge:]

Frank G.

John B.

[151: green sheet:]

words arising out of new promulgations of anything, ~~as of n physiology~~ – the words homœopathy and hydropathy — the various words of phrenology, – &c. &c ~~hydr~~

[152: blank]

[153: green sheet:]

forsat (for sä)     a convict

vendetta (feud – (Italian)

mirage (me –räźh)

---

| apres    (ä-pr)    adj | |
|---|---|
| rugged | tart |
| uneven | severe |
| rough (to touch) | pricky |
| harsh | fierce |
| sharp | violent |
| acrid | gruff |
| eager | greedy |
| ardent | voracious |

---

lorette – lo rèt     ("lady of easy virtue")

[154: blank]

[155: pale yellow sheet:]

for/ fort/

fort – forte – (Fr. adj)

| strong | large (in body, limb) |
|---|---|
| vigorous | considerable |
| stout | copious |
| sturdy | plentiful |

| | |
|---|---|
| hardy | great |
| lusty | intense |
| ~~strong~~ loud | vehement |
| energetic | able enough |
| spirited | powerful |
| brave | ready |
| courageous | capable |
| bold | hard |
| skilful | bad |
| cogent | violent |
| thick | coarse |
| of muscular fibre | hearty |
| a match for any thing | emphatic |
| (for animals, amours, | impressive |
| war, wit, learning) | severe |
| | valiant |
| | towering high |

~~fortement~~    fortment (adv.)
fortement        fr
    (for-te-mān)

[156: blank]

[157: pale yellow sheet:]
gavel–kind, – an old English custom, by which the lands of the father, at his
    death, were equally divided between all his sons
gavel, (an old English provincial word for <u>ground.</u>

redacteur ⎞ compiler
redactor  ⎬ <u>editor in chief</u>
          ⎟ <u>maker</u> up
redacter  ⎠ editor

[158: blank]

[159: pale yellow sheet:]
        New Names for Months

    In These States, there must be new Names for all the Months of the year
– They must be characteristic of America – The South, North, East, and West
must be represented in them –

What is the name ~~Juary~~ January to us? – Or March to us? – January ~~comes from~~ commemorates Janus – and March commemorates Mars – the bloody god of war, for the sake of War!

[160: blank]

[161: pale yellow sheet:]
   New Names for Counties

---

~~Most~~ Many of the Counties in the State—and ~~in all the Eastern~~ in other States — must be re–named

---

What is the name of Kings' County ~~to us~~? or of Queens County to us? — or St. Lawrence County?

---

Get rid as soon as convenient of all the bad names – not only of counties, rivers, towns, – but of persons, men and women –

[162: blank]

[163: pale yellow sheet:]
☞   The popular manly instinct, I notice, is continually trying to escape from Ephrainus and Johns and Rolando's – ? Whether Give to infants the names of qualities – physical and mental attributes. – Do not name them, till they exhibit these markedly – ? Whether Always select, of course, the most favorable phases of character – or of natural things – as Day, Hope, Oak, Rocky, ~~Trout~~, Fisherman, Sweet–breath

[164: pinned to the page is a full newspaper column, clipped, on 'Learning to Read by Phonotypy,' a method instigated in Waltham, Mass., by Thomas Rantey, encouraged by F. M. Stone, of their School Committee, and greatly favored by Cyrus Peirce.]

[165: pale yellow sheet:]
mal–address / bad address (evil luck in manners

---

malaprops (bad arrangements    unlucky steps

---

bizarreries (odd ways
        "    habits
        "    conduct

---

entrant (an tran)  ⎧insinuating
entrante (an trant)⎩ penetratingly winning⎭

---

entr' – (entre) (a useful prefix)
S'entr'admirier (s ā n trad-mi rá) (to admire one another)
(S)'entr'aimer (sān trè mé) (to love one another)

~~san~~

☞    entr' ⎧ between two or more
          ⎨ mixed with
          ⎩ merged – joined with

[166: blank]

[167: pale yellow sheet:]
corral ⎛ that is a pen, enclosure, over the southwest regions – at night, an
        ⎜ emigrant train of wagons, arranged in a hollow square, the cattle
        ⎝ inside in the corral, ⩇— or indeed any enclosure

[168: blank]

[169: pale yellow sheet:]
    exploit    (Fr
To exploit any thing – to make use of it (He exploits his courage, beauty, –
    viz: he puts them to the best advantage

[170: blank]

[171: pale yellow sheet:]

Physics
(Gr.)

| Physics (Gr.) | Metaphysics |
|---|---|
| All things – or the science of all things, materialistic, existing independently of the mind's conception of them — | Mental and spiritual things, as existing in and proceeding from the mind, the soul – or the science and study of such things — |
| The science of nature <br> – natural philosophy <br> – natural, not moral <br> – facts independent of the human will, or mental control | All that is not materialistic, but encloses the thought and amount of all materials – |
|  | All mind as distinguished from matter – |
| The objective of man | The subjective of man |

Physiology

All relating to or having <u>life</u>, or living action – Or the science of all
things generated or alive —
Vital phenomena, and all con-
nected with them — – all natural organization –
<u>Animal Physiology</u>, – of  animals –
Zoology
<u>Vegetable Physiology</u> – of vegetables
– Botany

"The science which regards the ulti-
mate grounds of being as dis-
tinguished from its phenomenal
modifications." <u>Brande</u>?
Intellectual Philosophy.
Ontology.
Psychology.
?All that is supernatural (!)

[172: blank]

[173: white scrap:]
see article "Ancient & Medieval India" p. 563   Eclectic May '70

[On yellow scrap pasted to white scrap:]
Mikkel Angelo.

Apollo Bel-vi-dar

[174: blank]

[175: pale yellow sheet:]

[Clipping:]

MEANINGS OF WORDS. — How many words men have dragged downwards
with themselves, and made partakers more or less of their own fall. Having
originally an honorable significance, they have yet, with the deterioration and
degeneration of those that used them, or those about whom they were used,
deteriorated or degenerated too. What a multitude of words, originally harm-
less, have assumed a harmful meaning as their secondary lease; how many
worthy have acquired an unworthy! Thus "knave" meant once no more than
a lad, (nor does it now in German mean more,) "villain" than peasant; a
"boor" was only a farmer, a "varlet" was but a serving man, a "menial" one
of the "many" or household, a "churl" but a strong fellow, a "minion" a favorite; man is "God's dearest minion," (Sylvester.) "Time-server" was used 200
years ago quite as often for one in an honorable as in a dishonorable sense,

"serving the time." "Conceits" had nothing once conceited in them; "officious" had reference to offices of kindness, and not of busy meddling; "moody" was that which pertained to a man's mood, without any gloom or sullenness implied. "Demure" ("des mœurs," of good manners,) conveyed no hint as it does now, of an overdoing of the outward demonstrations of modesty. In "crafty" and "cunning" there was nothing of crooked wisdom implied, but only knowledge and skill; "craft," indeed, still retains very often its more honorable use, a man's "craft" being his skill, and then the trade in which he is well skilled. And think you that the Magdalen could have ever given us "maudlin" in its present contemptuous application, if the tears of penitential weeping had been held in due honor by the world?

[176: blank]

[177: rough lined scrap glued (reading upwards) on a pale yellow sheet:]
Words    bona fides
—

. . . . "You must be the judge of the bona fides of the man" . . .

[178: blank]

[179: lined scrap on a pale yellow sheet:]
ŏ as foot
contretemps – (against time)
    kŏn-tr-tóng –
    — an accidental occurrence or something that confuses & mars every thing —

[180: blank]

[181: blank]

[182: blank]

[183: blank]

[184: blank]

[185: blank]

[186: blank]

[187: white sheet:]

Names of cities, islands, rivers, new settlements, &c. These should/ must assimilate in sentiment and in sound, to something organic in the place, or identical with it. — It is far better to call a new inhabited island ,by the native word, than by its first discoverer, or to call it New anything. — Aboriginal names always tell finely; sometimes it is necessary to slightly Anglicise them. — All classic names are objectionable. How much better Ohio, Oregon, Missouri, Milwaukee &c. Iowa [?] than New York, Ithaca, Naples, &c. —

[188: blank]

[189: very small Williamsburgh tax form, blue:]
Albany originally indicates the sense of ~~wholeness~~ w white color or of partial
    transparency

[190: blank]

[Clipping tipped in:]

### ORIGIN OF THE NAMES OF STATES.

MAINE was so called as early as 1623, from Maine, in France, of which Henrietta Maria, Queen of England, was at that time proprietor.

NEW HAMPSHIRE was the name given to the territory conveyed by the Plymouth Company, to Captain John Mason, by patent, Nov. 7th, 1629, with reference to the patentee, who was Governor of Portsmouth, in Hampshire, England.

VERMONT was so called by the inhabitants in their Declaration of Independence, Jan. 16th, 1777, from the French, *verd mont* (the green mountain).

MASSACHUSETTS was so called from Massachusetts Bay, and that from the Massachusetts tribe of Indians in the neighborhood of Boston. The tribe is thought to have derived its name from the Blue Hills of Milton. "I had learnt," says Roger Williams, "that the Massachusetts were so called from the Blue Hills."

RHODE ISLAND was so called, in 1664, in reference to the Island of Rhodes in the Mediterranean.

CONNECTICUT was so called from the Indian name of its principal river. Connecticut is a Mocheakanneew word, signifying *long river*.

NEW YORK was so called in 1664, in reference to the Duke of York and Albany, to whom this territory was granted by the King of England.

NEW JERSEY was so called in 1664, from the Island of Jersey on the coast of France, the residence of the family of Sir George Carteret, to whom the territory was granted.

PENNSYLVANIA was so called in 1681, after William Penn.

DELAWARE was so called in 1703, from Delaware Bay, on which it lies, and which received its name from Lord de la War, who died in this bay.

MARYLAND was so called in honor of Henrietta Maria, Queen of Charles I, in his patent to Lord Baltimore, June 30, 1632.

VIRGINIA was so called in 1584, after Elizabeth, the virgin Queen of England.

CAROLINA was so called by the French in 1564, in honor of King Charles IX., of France.

GEORGIA was so called in 1732, in honor of King George II.

ALABAMA was so called in 1814, from its principal river, it being an Indian name, signifying *here we rest.*

MISSISSIPPI was so called in 1800, from its western boundary. Mississippi is said to denote the *whole river,* i.e., the river formed by the union of many.

LOUISIANA was so called in honor of Louis XIV., of France.

TENNESSEE was so called in 1796, from its principal river. The word Ten-asse is said to signify a *curved spoon.*

KENTUCKY was so called in 1792; the word is of native origin, and signifies the *dark and bloody ground.*

ILLINOIS was so called in 1809, from its principal river. The word is said to signify *the river of men.*

INDIANA was so called in 1809, from the American Indians.

OHIO was so called in 1802, from its southern boundary.

MISSOURI was so called in 1821, from its principal river.

MICHIGAN was so called in 1805, from the lake on its border.

ARKANSAS was so called in 1812, from its principal river.

FLORIDA was so called by Juan Ponce de Leon, in 1572, because it was discovered on Easter Sunday; in Spanish, *Pascua Florida.*

COLUMBIA was so called in reference to Columbus.

WISCONSIN was so called from its principal river.

IOWA was so called from its principal river.

OREGON was so called from its principal river.

MINNESOTA; or, the Wandering Water.

[191: small white scrap:]
America of course needs ~~new names~~ New Names for the Months
as for instance ~~what~~ how absurd our name of "September,") – seventh
    month from the Roman — (The Roman year beginning in March)

[192: blank]

[Clipping tipped in:]

And here the occurrence of the words "lady and "ladies" in three books of the Old Testament and one of the New, in the English translation of the Bible, (in all six times, while "woman" and "women," *I find by the Concordance,* occur not far from two hundred and fifty times,) confirms my view of the subject; for in every one of those five or six cases, as I learn from a friend acquainted with the originals, the Hebrew and Greek words really imply station, authority and power — sometimes sovereign power — and in no one of them simply "woman."

In fact the word "lady" in English, (whatever the etymology, which is a matter of dispute,) is certainly the feminine of "lord." It originally implied — and when used in our admirable translation of the Bible it unquestionably implied — rank, dignity, and station. As the mind willingly transfers to eminent moral worth the appellatives of eminent station, the term may still be properly applied to those admirable women in every rank of life who "derive their patent of nobility from Heaven." It also has its appropriate place in the metaphorical language of rhetoric, poetry, pleasantry, and satire, of which last I quoted two striking examples in my former communication to the *Intelligencer.* But I remain of the opinion that, for every purpose of civility, respect, or affection, in public address or private intercourse, "woman" is by far the simpler, kindlier, and more expressive term; and, therefore, *"young women"* for the single, and *"matrons"* for the married, (*mater, mothers,*) are my usual terms of address for these whom we cannot honor too much — nor enough.

And now, gentlemen, though "man that is born of *woman* is of few days and full of trouble," I think I shall not again trouble you on the subject.

Respectfully,                              THOMAS H. BENTON.

[193: blue Williamsburgh tax form:]
Bailey's Dictionary, about 1728
Johnson's Dictionary first published 1755
Worcester says that no other work ever had so great an influence on the
        English Language as it.

| | | | |
|---|---|---|---|
| Julius Cesar landed in Britain | } | B. C. 55 | |
| Saxons invaded it | } | Middle 5<sup>th</sup> | Century A. C. |
| Norman invasion William the Conquerer | } | 1066 | A. C. |

[194: blank]

[195: pale yellow sheet:]

[Clipping:]

*Change in the Meaning of Words.* — A contemporary collates from French, the following interesting explanation of the change and original signification of many words in our language, in common use: An interesting fact in regard to our language, is the great change which has taken place in the meaning of many words. The word "miscreant," which now means "a vile wretch," in Shakspere's time meant simply a misbeliever; and when Talbot calls "Joan of Arc," a miscreant, he intends to intimate that she has fallen from the faith. How many are aware that the word "influence," as used by the earlier English poets, had a more or less remote allusion to the influences which the heavenly bodies were supposed to exercise upon men? "Baffled," which means defeated, was applied in the days of chivalry to a recreant knight, who was either in person or in effigy, hung up by his heels, his escutcheon blotted, his spear broken, and himself or his effigy subjected to all kinds of indignities. "Nephews," as used by Hooker, Shakspere, and other writers of the Elizabethan period, denoted grand-children and other lineal descendants. "Kindly fruits," as used in the Litany, also simply denotes the natural fruits, or those which the earth, according to its kind, should naturally bring forth. A historian, speaking of a celebrated divine who had recently died, exclaimed, "Oh the painfulness of his preaching!" by which he did not mean that his preaching was painful to his hearers, but that he bestowed much labor and pains upon the preparation of his sermons. The term "meat" was formerly applied to all food, but is now restricted to flesh only. Not a few words were once applicable to both sexes, which are now restricted to the female; as an illustration, the word "girl" may be mentioned, which formerly denoted a young person of either sex. Under the reign of Edward the First, the word "acre" meant any field of whatever size. "Furlong" denoted the length of a furrow; or a "furrow-long." Also the words "yard," "peck," and "gallon" were once of a vague and unsettled use, and only at a later day, and in obedience to the requirements of commerce and social life, were they used to denote exact measures and designations.

[196: blank]

[197: pale yellow sheet:]

[Clipping of an article, one paragraph, on "Specimen of Phonetic Printing",

which is here reproduced with its "phonetic" letters; Whitman's notation
reads:      Phonetic Journal May 1886

SPESIMEN OV FONETIK PRINTIU.

For tuu hundred yirz after de introdukcon ov printiŋ, der
woz no standard ov orbografi, but everi printer speld az aimd
reit in hiz on ciz.  de konsekwens woz dat no tuu printerz
speld aleik.  de publik konviniens demanded a yuniform
orbografi, and tordz de end ov de seventinb sentiuri, de orbografi woz seteld (wid fiu eksepconz,) az wi nou hav it.
But it woz seteld on a roŋ foundccon—an imperfekt alfabet.
de introdukcon ov a fonetik alfabet and orbografi, haz ekiu-
peid de atencon ov meni ov de gretest nemz in iŋglic literatiur,
"Suner or leter," sez Dr Fraŋklin, " it must bi dun, or our
reitiŋ wil bikum de sem az de teeiniz (Chinese), az tu de difi-
kulti ov lerniŋ and yuuziŋ it; and it wud olredi hav bin suto
if wi had kontiniud de sakson speliŋ and reitiŋ yuuzd bei our
forfaderz."

The Mormons of Utah are using the phonography in print

## "Indian"

Of course the word "Indian" does not belong apply to the American
aborigines. — It originated – An Indian is a man or woman of the lower
southern and eastern half of Asia. It confuses and vexes language to have
these such synonyms with contra–meanings.


[198: blank]


[199: small blue Williamsburgh tax form:]
       Words Wanted

---

A word which happily expresses the idea of
       An Equal Friend of All These States

---

Because this is a word to express what must be become a distinct class of persons here perhaps now arising.


[200: blank]


[201: pale yellow sheet:]
word to be introduced
       plaza (Sp)    for public ground – city square or park

[202: blank]

[203: pale yellow sheet:]
plentiful crops of words, or new applications of words arising out of the general establishment and use of new inventions, ~~becoming~~ such as the words ~~of~~ from the steam–engine, and its various moving and stationary structures, on land and water – words from the electric telegraph, the sewing–machine, the daguerreotype, the modern ~~daily~~ ⤷ newspaper press

Many of the above are words of <u>Personnel</u> — of the names applied to the men and women who have to do with the new inventions. —

[204: blank]

[205: pale yellow sheet:]
varmint (from vermin)

[206: blank]

[207: slip (written upwards) of white lined paper:]
<u>schema</u> — (the entire <u>schema</u> or set of propositions.)
        "<u>th</u>e <u>schema ad Fidem</u>"

[208: blank]

[209: pale yellow sheet:]
? Companions

─────

? Walt Whitmans Companions

[210: blank]

[211: pale yellow sheet:]
    Phonographic short hand

I notice often the reporters about Brooklyn and New York using phonographic short-hand. They say it is very useful to them, enabling them to give verbatim reports of any thing spoken or read. — It requires a practice of two, three, or more years to be perfect. —

[212: blank]

[213: blank]

[214: very narrow strip (written upwards) pasted on yellow sheet:]
("got a dote on" as the drivers say —

[215: broad slip of white lined paper:]
x x x he said of ~~the~~ great fat young B –
    – "he has too much
      slush-muscle about him"

[216: blank]

[217: blank]

[218: blank]

[219: pale blue Williamsburgh tax form (verso, as before:]
Caxton, (first English printer)  }  1480
Translation of Eneid, in English  ;  1490

---

☞   Phrase Book  ☜
   Is not a Phrase Book, ~~now~~ An American one, just as much needed as a
Dictionary? —

---

        (The above is a hint for the New Dictionary)

[220: blank]

[221: pale yellow sheet:]
     kosmical
(Prof. Olmstead says of the aurora borealis "I consider it kosmical in its
origin — not terrestial.")

---

   entourage (n m) (– an tour azh)    – railing round a theatre &c persons
        around any one
(sc of)    entourer     (v a)   (an tour a) de (with)   of
          to surround – to close in – to wreath (as with a garland)

[222: blank]

[223: verso of blue Williamsburgh tax form, small part:]
    Lessons
Onward    Lessons
Passing      "
Initiative
Primary
Starting

---

  American Lessons

    ☞

Arousing Lessons
Hints and Lessons
    Walt Whitman's Lessons
Travelling Lessons

[224: blank]

[225: verso of blue Williamsburgh tax form, small part:]
American Lessons ~~In-Transitu~~
              In–Transitu
Transcendental Lessons
Original Lessons
First      "
Parturition   "
Lessons Accouché
   ☞

[226: blank]

[227: pale yellow sheet:]
   in Names – a suggestion
The woman should preserve her own name, just as much after marriage as
    before

---

Also all titles must be dropped — no ~~Mrs~~ Mr. or Mrs. or Miss any more

[228: blank]

[229: pale blue Williamsburgh tax form, verso:]
   500 years ago

Statute Edward 3ᵈ that pleas should be in the ⎫
    English tongue (not Norman French ⎬ 136[0]
⎭

(This is the date of the author[ized] formation of the English lang[uage] as
    we have it now.

---

In this century (13–1400) flo[urished]
    Chaucer       Wickliffe
    Sir John Mandeville

---

    No. of words)
Edinburgh Review says 38,000
— But Johnson's Dictionary    as xxxxx[?] him, has more than that

[230: blank]

[231: pale yellow sheet:]
    ignoramii
    ignoramus

the common people say of nourishing food that "it stays with a man."

[232: blank]

[233: verso of pale blue Williamsburgh tax form:]
    Webster's Introduction.

---

Changes from Anglo Saxon since the Norman Conquest

---

the substitution of k for c as "look" for locian –
the loss of h before l as "loaf" for "hlaf" — "lot" for "hlot"
the loss of the prefix "ge" or "ga" — as "deal" now, instead of "ge-dælan"
the similar loss of "to" — as now we write "help" for the old "to–helpan"
also the plural termination "en" has been generally dropt, as now "houses"
    for the old "housen"

---

"if" from the Saxon "gif" or give — as – "If ~~that~~ a man knows his true in-
    terest, he will avoid a quarrel" —
    viz: "Gif <u>that</u> a man" &c – i e Give that
— always then the "if" is equivalent to "Give that" so and so.

---

Webster says of the subjunctive mood, the current dandyfied form is all amiss
☞    see p    liii (53) Introduction

[234: blank]

[235: pale yellow sheet:]

      in Spanish (at Lima &c) diminutives in the names of persons, for endearment   <u>ita</u> } & ( <u>ito</u> )
        for fem } & ( for males )
        ales }

---

      "plunder" (i. e.)
          miscellaneous goods

[236: blank]

[237: verso of pale blue Williamsburgh tax form:]
      Webster's Introduction

---

    He gives specimens of the Saxon (Anglo Saxon) as used before the Norman conquest – viz:
      from the Saxon Chronicle, A D 891 & from
          the Laws of King Ethelbert &
          "  "  "  " Edgar
This, with some words introduced by the Danes, continued to be used by the English till the Norman conquest (   ) ~~after~~ since which great numbers of Saxon words ~~went~~ have gone out of use (perhaps half) — and French & Latin words were added by degrees, till <u>it began to assume its present</u> form, in the 14$^{th}$ & 15$^{th}$ Centuries

---

— (Yet Gower & Chaucer cannot now be understood without a glossary)

---

<u>Changes also in sounds – of vowels</u>
<u>a</u> probably in old times had generally the sound of <u>a</u> in <u>fall</u> and sometimes of
    <u>a</u> in <u>far</u> — not at all our sound of <u>a</u> in <u>make</u>: — this last sound belonged
    generally to <u>e – i</u> was our present <u>ee</u>   long <u>u</u> was <u>oo</u> —

[238: blank]

[239: small white sheet:]
    The history of any country or age, is contained in a string of its names, as
Rome by
Greece by
Assyria

Egypt
The Jews
The Dark Ages
America
The geography of
        the earth by

[240: blank]

[241: verso of pale blue Williamsburgh tax form:]
        Webster's Introduction                    a good word
                                                          radix
_____

"Consonants are the Stamina of Words"
            ( ? the bones of words)
_____

"Mons. Gebelin, in his <u>Monde Primitif</u> says the Noun is the root of the other
        words. — Never was a greater mistake. — That some nouns may be, is
        possible — but, as languages are now constructed, it is demonstrable
        that the verb is the radix or stock from which have sprung most of the
        nouns, adjectives, and other parts of speech belonging to the same
        family. This is the result of all my researches into the origin of lan-
        guages"
_____

(Me, W. W. I think with the Frenchman that nouns begin the matter. —
        Language may have since been scraped and drenched down to the
        completer state, which makes the verbs the centres, for grammatical
        purposes; but, in the nature of things, nouns must have been first, and
        essentially remain so. —

[242: blank]

[243: verso of pale blue Williamsburgh tax form:]
        Websters Introduction
_____

After the Conquest, the Norman kings strove to extirpate the English Lan-
        guage, and substitute the Norman. – It was ordained that the law records
        & proceedings should be in Norman

After 300 years, a change, and to the other tack. —
Thus a portion of Norman words remain in English, mainly law–words.
_____

        The English then is <u>a Composite of</u>
1ˢᵗ  Saxon & Danish words of Teutonic or Gothic origin

2$^d$  British, Welsh, &c.-viz: Celtic
3$^d$  Norman, (a mixture of French & Gothic)
4$^{th}$ Latin, (formed on Celtic & Teutonic)
5$^{th}$ French (chiefly Latin corrupted)
6$^{th}$ Greek (Celtic & Teutonic, with some Coptic)
7$^{th}$ Italian, Spanish, German, &c.
8$^{th}$ a few foreign words introduced by commerce, or political or literary neces-
sities.
Of these the Saxon is the trunk. — The Danish & Welsh also are primitive
words, and part of our vernacular — of equal antiquity with Chaldee
and Syriac

[244: blank]

[245: verso of pale blue Williamsburgh tax form:]
        Websters Introduction.

German, Dutch, or Belgic, Anglo–Saxon, Danish & Swedish languages are
of Teutonic or Gothic origin

*Note– In strictness the Swedish & Danish are Gothic — the German and
Saxon Teutonic

remains of Celtic – The purest remains
are the     Basque in Spain
            Gaelic, north Scotland
            Hibernian, in Ireland

English, (as now written)
        the basis Saxon – (Anglo Saxon)
        but retaining a great many words from the ancient languages of Britain,
        especially the Welsh (or Cymraey) — containing also many words in-
        troduced by the Danes, (Gothic) who were for some time masters of
        England

[246: blank]

[247: verso of pale blue Williamsburgh tax form:]
        Webster's Dict.    Introduction
Of the languages of Europe, the Greek was first improved and refined, and
next to that the Latin. —

Probably some words in the Greek were derived from Africa — as doubtless there were Egyptian colonies established in Greece.

| The Modern Italian | |
| Spanish | are composed chiefly of Latin words, much altered, however, both in orthography and inflections |
| French | |
| & Portuguese | |

Perhaps nine–tenths of the words in those languages are of Latin words–roots — Rome having held Gaul as a province for six centuries, and Spain still longer

Still the above have terms from Celtic word–roots. —

[248: blank]

[249: verso of pale blue Williamsburgh tax forms:]
p lxii          Webster's Introduction

Lindley Murray follows "Lowth's Principles"

"Comptroller"

Webster shows ~~his a most dg dog~~ a stiff–necked obstinacy sometimes — as in the word "Comptroller" — which he says is unquestionably a stupid blunder, and should be "Controler" or "Controller," from conte-role, French, a duplicate roll or list kept to check accounts. — It is, however, more likely that we have the word from the Latin, whence compute, computation, accomp't, ~~acct~~ &c., to count — and that the old way is the best. — It is also an argument in its favor that "Comptroler" is a specific word for the head finance–man, while "Controler" —

[250: blank]

[251: verso of pale blue Williamsburgh tax form:]
Equal <u>Antiquity of English</u>

In reality the English Language, in its body or stock, is of just as great antiquity as the Greek, the Roman, or any of the languages of Asia. — The assumptions of lexicographers that certain of our words are "derived" from similar words are worth just as much, and is about as sensible as the assertion that I am derived from my ~~brothers or sisters, or from my~~ father's side cousins ~~or~~ because we bear the same name. —

☞ Common stock

[252: blank]

[253: verso of pale blue Williamsburgh tax form:]
    ☞ ~~Webster certainly~~

---

Webster's ~~horrible~~ sickish Boston pronunciation of ä in mäst, ╲läughter, &c ~~instead of a as in "bare," "mare"~~ ~~like the a sound~~ ~~in~~ "~~where~~" He leaves out altogether that rich sound of a like the dwelt–upon and prolonged ~~sounds~~ tone of ~~a~~ the middle letter of "sad" "man" viz. ⌿ "sa-h-d" man — Webster does not know the sound, nor give any mark to it. — ? bare, mare,

---

digraph – union of two vowels, in which only one is pronounced
    (the German is full of this)

[254: blank]

[255: small salmon slip:]
    Language follows events, ~~a~~ and swallows them to preserve them. — Conquests, migrations, commerce, &c are fossilized in language.

[256: blank]

[257: verso of pale blue Williamsburgh tax form:]
    Webster ~~certainly~~ unquestionably ~~had a~~ lacked ~~a good~~ ear, ~~1 To a stranger of ⌿ The~~ and his Dictionary does after him — a fatal defect. — The maker of a Dictionary ~~should~~ need not be a musician, but must be a master or mistress of musicians. — ~~he or she~~ For our English language ~~is a no-less~~ overarches ~~should and~~ all music ~~greater~~ and is greater than all the compositions played by instruments or sung by trained singers. — This is ~~not~~ no ~~one-of-the-care~~ thoughtless flight✕ of the rhyme–poets, but a ~~stron~~ provable fact.

[258: blank]

[259: small scrap of a Williamsburgh tax form:]
Manhatta (or Monhatta) – (A peninsular island, ~~sur~~ enclosed by active, ~~and~~
    changing or playful waters. —
Mä na hätta

[260: blank]

[261: salmon colored sheet:]

(Bunsen)    (p 240)        Hebrew

"From the Egyptian researches the art of writing and historical records existed long prior to the time of Moses and the Exodus — (14ᵗʰ century before Christ)

A link or chain onward and downward a thousand years)

1000  years

Moses — Judges (song of Deborah) — Haggai — Malachi — Ecclesiastes, &c.

(Geography — Goodrich

About Eighty original languages — with 3000 dialects)

Hebrew affords monuments of higher    antiquity than Arabic or Ethiopic.

The Hebrew traditions, (from the conservative character of the race,) have
    been far better preserved than those of any other people.
What an illustration of mental and spiritual ru[le] through lang[uage] is the
    Hebrew.

[262: blank]

[263: smaller salmon colored sheet:]

| | | |
|---|---|---|
| | Sanscrit, | |
| | Old Persian, | |
| Japhetic | Greek, | |
| languages | Latin, | |
| ——— | Lithuanian | |
| also ⎫ Indo– | Sclavonic | |
| called ⎭ Teutonic | Teutonic | (in its ancient dialect, the Gothic. |
| ꝑ also | Celtic | |
| ᐧ Iranian? | | |

Sidon, a city    the Phenician Metropolis    (Canaan
                                viz. Palestine)
                        when Abraham "squatted" there

Phenician language may be called a tissue of which Hebrew forms the woof
    and Syrian the warp

[264: blank]

[265: salmon colored sheet:]

The Indo–European languages (Japhetic) ?Iranian offer undeniable proof of the gradual extension of races from the eastern part of Central Asia

---

The Semitic present no less striking evidence of being derived from the western portion of the same ~~Asiatic~~ continental and primitive seat of mankind.

(Bunsen page 178)

---

Semitic ~~languages~~ tribes, in western Asia, and penetrating into Africa, both along the Mediterranean, and down through the interior

---

? The Arabic seems to be the most ancient branch of the <u>Semitic</u>, and the Hebrew follows it

---

Rusk proved that Finnic (?Scythian) had once been spok[en] on the northern extremities of Europe, and t[he] allied languages extended like a girdle over northern Asia, Europe, and America

Rusk proposed the following division of the <u>Scythian</u> race
    1  North Asiatic        3  Tartar
    2  North American       4  Mongol or Tu[?]
A later authority leaves out the N. A.

[266: blank]

[267: smaller salmon colored sheet:]
The Celtic has a higher claim to antiquity than the Teutonic (or Gothic)
— (~~Bunsen thinks it anterior to the Sanscrit, also~~)
— Bunsen thinks it occupies, in history, a place between the Sanskrit and the Egyptian.

---

(Bunsen) on written Language
"Do not forget that what is now fixed was once floating and movable."

---

(me)
What science, what music, what a development, in the modern alphabet!

[268: blank]

[269: salmon colored sheet:]
    W. Von Humboldt
— that language is the outward expression of wha[t] he calls the spirit or individuality of a nation. —

☞

Von Humboldt
"Language expresses originally objects only, and leaves the understanding to supply the connecting form — afterwards facilitating and improving the connections and relations by degrees.

Bunsen
(Chinese he calls a "family language)    The old Chinese has a style such as only a solitary thinker could frame in his conversations with himself – a kind of algebraic chain, intelligible to the initiated, but not to others. — Chinese is therefore admirably fitted to meditation and reflection. — It is a language of Brahmanic Musings, but unfit for the forum

[270: blank]

[271: narrow salmon colored sheet:]

Bunsen p 350    English, as well as Dutch and Frisic, belongs to the Low
Arian    German branch — This, with High German and Scandinavian, a branch of the T

Teutonic   stock, which with
Celtic
Slavonic
Hellenic    are members of the Arian
Italic    family — (making English
Iranic &    also a member)
Indic

[272: blank]

[273: narrow salmon colored sheet:]
    ? of Swinton
What are the Turanian languages?

    Arian –(Greek)
Turanian, (Turk)

Semitic, (Hebrew.)

{ "Arian Brahman"
The Arian seem to be those that have
flowed out, or have an allied character
with the Hindustan, the Sanskrit, ~~the~~
"~~Dekhan~~", — the land of the Indus and
the Ganges —

What the Arian
The Arians were
the higher classes,
later–comers, con-
querors of India-as
the Normans, under
William the Conqueror,
in England — They were
the Brahmanic Caste

[274: blank]

[275: narrow salmon colored sheet:]
In Southern Asia there are distinct dialects spoken by only forty or fifty families — so that although surrounded by neighbors, ~~the~~ verbal communication
with them is difficult

Sanskrit,
Persian
Greek,
Latin,
Sclavonic,
Teutonic &
Celtic,

are simply <u>continuations of</u>
<u>one common</u> spring of Language

~~as~~

as

Spanish,
Portuguese,
French,
Provençal,
Italian &
Wallachian

are <u>all</u> but
<u>Latin</u>
under different
aspects.

[276: in pencil:]

– but how much further back no one can tell, although
certainly very much further [refers to the comment on bottom of p. 277]

[277: smaller salmon colored sheet:]

(me   (I believe) /

Thus individualism is ~~seen~~ a law in modern languages, and freedom also. —
The words are not built in, but stand loose, and ready to go this way
or that.

---

(Bunsen)

The modern alphabet ~~has~~ dates back ~~also~~ very far — perhaps 10 000 years
perhaps 20,000.

~~The Phenician was a from   Th Now perfected from~~ ~~the Phenician,~~ Clearly
[?]
traced to the Phenician, the Phenician also is traced to such and more
ancient stages previous

[278: blank]

[279: smaller salmon sheet:]

( Bunsen p 165–6 )

The marked difference in the way by which modern languages as different
from ancient languages, express the application, modification, variation,
connection, ~~and~~ &c. of the main ideas of a sentence

–As  :

( in English &c. by <u>auxiliaries</u>
( — in Latin &c. by inflexions —
( i.e. suffixes and prefixes

Horse . . . . man – death.

---

made up by conjunctions, prepositions, articles &c.

~~The~~        any way we please

The horse kicked the man to death. The man rode the horse to death, & in
more than a hundred different ways all with three leading nouns

---

The ancient Greek and Latin seem to have affected these connections by
terminations

[280: blank]

[Tipped in here is a long clipping, in two parts, of a meeting where several
papers on language were read; one of the paragraphs has been encircled:]

Dr. McIlvaine thought that the language of a nation was the natural expression of its thought and life, and if a nation were to adopt a new language
it would ruin its development.

[281: small salmon colored sheet:]

Walt
Whitman's $\begin{cases} \text{Primer–Less} \\ \text{Starting lessons} \\ \text{Train–Lessons} \\ \text{Beginnings} \end{cases}$

? Or is not simply

– – : Lessons better than any or all of the rest

[282: blank:]

[Tipped in here is a clipping from a magazine, with a notation in the margin in WW's hand:]

Died
1846
Language

[The comment refers to John Pickering, in the paragraph, which has been tipped in:]

May 5. — In Boston, Mass., *Hon. John Pickering, LL.D.,* President of the American Academy of Arts and Sciences, aged 69. He was a son of the late Timothy Pickering, so much distinguished in the political history of this country, and was born in Salem, Mass., where he resided till a late period of his life. He was educated at Harvard College, where he graduated in 1796. He entered into active life as a lawyer, and obtained much distinction as an able jurist and also as a politician, having served for several years as a member of the senate of Massachusetts. But his reputation rests chiefly on his attainments as a scholar and on his literary and scientific labors, which were of great service to the cause of learning in this country. His studies related chiefly to philology, and in this department he was excelled by no American, except perhaps the late Mr. Duponceau. His chief publications were a vocabulary of Americanisms, and a Greek and English Lexicon, the first on the largest scale, we believe, which was ever published in this country. He studied thoroughly the aboriginal languages of America, and was acquainted to some extent with the Oriental tongues. He held the office of president of the Oriental Society at Boston, at the time of his death. He marked out the plan for reducing to writing the language of the Sandwich Islanders. His other labors are too numerous and important to be noticed in this sketch. In all the relations of private and public life, he commanded the respect and esteem of his friends and the whole community.

[Tipped in here is a long clipping, in two parts, "A Word on Spelling", a letter to *The New York Tribune,* by Elizur Wright, dated 22 July 1857.]

[283: small scrap, verso of a pale blue Williamsburgh tax form:]
　　Words remain in use, sometimes very inappropriately — as the word "peti-
tion," so generally applied to ~~paper~~ requests, papers, &c sent to Congress, State
Legislatures, and Common Councils, — the better word is "Memorial," or
"Application," or Statement."

[284: blank]

[285: slightly larger verso of pale blue Williamsburgh tax form:]
　　Is not the most exquisite delicacy of the use of words, in that of <u>adjectives</u>?

———————

The nouns take care of themselves — the verbs also, though not so much as
　　　　the nouns — But in the use of <u>adjectives</u> is a great art –　　(Style is
　　　　shown in the use on non–use  of adjectives) – a great choice
Trace adjectives to their roots – as tortuous cereal.
— Track adjectives ~~like~~ closely to their roots, and literal meanings before
　　using them. —

[286: blank]

[287: verso of a small piece of pale blue Williamsburgh tax form:]
　　　　Tracing words to origins

——————————————

To get in the habit of tracing words to their root–meanings –
　　　　as for instance in the phrase "Rev. Mr. Conway" trace "Reverend"
　　　　　　　　　　　　　　　　　　　　　　　　　"    "Mr."
　　　　– how inapplicable and superfluous so many words are!

[288: blank]

[289: small white lined slip of paper:]
"Vivat hoch (ve-vat hō) "hoch"
　　　　　　　　　　　(i.e) high
"Es lebe die Freiheit"
　　live　　　　freedom
　? lē bē　(fri-hite)

[290: blank]

[291: pale yellow sheet:]
    Names

for the U. S        } The Small House or Branch
    Senate          }     of Congress
For the           } The Large House of
    Representatives }   Congress

The two –    The Houses of Congress

                    or simply
                    The Congress

[Clipping:]

DISTINGUISHED VISITERS AT WASHINGTON. — The Federal Capital is full of "Ingins," among whom are Wa-ga-sup-pa, the Iron Whip; Tish-ta-wa-go, Charles Chief; Wash-kom-ma-na, Hard Walker; Shoo-cob-a, Heavy Cloud; Ish-ga-ne-kai-ba, Love Chief; Shang-gis-ka, White Horse; and Tah-tang-ga-na-tha, Standing Buffalo — all braves of the Poncas tribe, and splendid-built fellows, standing six feet and upwards in their moccasins.

[292: blank]

[293: verso of a small piece of pale blue Williamsburgh tax-form:]
    Pantaloons for men were ~~only~~ introduced into America from France about the commencement of the present century

[Clipping pinned to sheet:]

Dress in the Olden Time. — In the days of Washington, says a writer in *Putnam's Magazine* for February, clothing was very expensive; and though made a matter of more consequence than now, as marking the distinctions of rank, sedulously maintained, it was often difficult for persons of much pretension to keep up the outward appearance of gentility. For this reason all apparel was preserved with much care. I have seen specimens of mending, piecing, and darning in garments belonging to old families which would have commanded a premium from some of our modern industrial societies. The raiment purchased for a young woman's bridal was worn by her in old age; and young girls of the household were glad to assume the faded relics of a grandmother's wardrobe. Rich dresses, in those days, were considered of sufficient importance to be mentioned in wills, and left, as an inheritance to relatives or friends.

[294: blank]

[Several leaves, stubs, and fly-leaves: nothing attached but few words in Whitman's hand. Pinned or placed in the book, the exact place not known now, are five clippings from newspapers (3), a magazine, and a book: "The English and French Languages"; "Unity of the Human Organism", *The New York Tribune,* April 12?, 1861; "A New System of Primary Instruction", *The New York Tribune,* March 30?, 1861; "[Addison on] [3438] The English Language", pp. 239–241 (of ? ); "The Spirit of the Age: The Late Mr. Horne Tooke", pp. 73–77, with Whitman marginalia on pp. 73–74:] Horne Tooke on Language — something on etymology — and something on profounder topics

☞ These 3 leaves encompass *the whole matter.*

Also ~~of words, of him who~~ no man can really understand words, except [ ? ] and rarely will one be met who has [ ? ] and which the grammarians and lexicographers, so far, have not one of them had. —

---

3438.   These two words, "Addison on," are in Whitman's hand.

平

The Primer Of Words[3439]

~~For American~~

For American Young, Men, and Women,

For Literats,

Orators,

Teachers,

Musicians,

Judges

Presidents,

&c[3440]

3439. The published version of this material is entitled, by its editor, *An American Primer*, by Walt Whitman, *With Facsimiles of the Original Manuscript*, edited by Horace Traubel (Boston: Small, Maynard & Company, 1904, ix, 35 pp.), issued in a limited edition of 500 copies, the format, type, and binding similar to *Walt Whitman's Diary in Canada*. It has since been reprinted, photographically, by City Lights Books, San Francisco, 1970; and by the Folcroft Press, Folcroft, Pennsylvania, 1969. Three pages are reproduced, in color, between the foreword and the text. The text in the current edition is here reproduced from the 110-page MS in the Feinberg Collection and with its original title, "The Primer of Words." The pages are not numbered, but I have supplied numbers in square brackets. The Foreword, by Horace Traubel, set in italics, pp. v–ix, reads:

The American Primer is a challenge rather than a finished fight. We find Whitman on this occasion rather laying his plans than undertaking to perfect them. It would be unfair to take such a mass of more or less disjointed notes and pass them under severe review. Whitman never intended them for publication. He should not be criticised, as he has been by certain American editors, for an act for which he is in no way responsible. The Primer is not a dogma. It is an interrogation. Even as a dogma something might be said for it. As a question it intimates its own answer. One of Whitman's remarks about it was this: "It does not suggest the invention but describes the growth of an American English enjoying a distinct identity." Whitman would every now and then get on his financial uppers. Then he would say: "I guess I will be driven to the lecture field in spite of myself." The Primer was one of his projected lecture themes. The lecture idea had possessed him most convincingly in the period that antedated our personal acquaintance. *Leaves of Grass* appeared before I was born. When I got really into contact with Whitman the fight was on in its full fury. "The Leaves has always meant fight to the world. It never meant fight to me." That was what Whitman said of it. He would make a point of my youth. "You bring young blood to the field. We are veterans — we welcome you."

Whitman at different times, especially in the beginning, when he struck up his rebel

What is the ~~strange charm our~~ fitness — what the ~~fitness~~ strange charm of aboriginal names. — Monongahela (rep) – it rolls with venison upon the palate

A perfect user of words uses things – ~~they~~ the exude ~~A p~~ in power and beauty from him – Miracles from his hands — miracles from his mouth – ~~things,~~ things, lilies, clouds, sunshine, women, poured [ ? ]iously —

note, planned for all sorts of literary ventures which were not consummated. Whitman was undoubtedly convinced that he had a mission. This conviction never assumed fanatic forms. Whitman was the most catholic man who ever thought he had a mission. But he did regard himself as such a depository. Yet he never believed or contended that he · possessed exclusive powers or an extraordinary divination. He felt that if the message with which he was entrusted did not get out through him it would get out through some other. But in his earlier career, after he tired of writing in the formal way and to the formal effect — for he played the usual juvenile part in literary mimicry — he felt that it would be difficult, if not impossible, to secure publishers either for his detail work or for his books. He often asked himself: How am I to deliver my goods? He once decided that he would lecture. And he told me that when the idea of The American Primer originally came to him it was for a lecture. Yet these notes in themselves were only fragments. He never looked upon them as furnishing more than a start. "They might make the material for a good talk," he said. "It's only a sketch-piece anyway," he said again: "a few rough touches here and there, not rounding up the theme — rather showing what may be made of it. I often think the Leaves themselves are much the same sort of thing: a passage way to something rather than a thing in itself concluded: not the best that might be done but the best it is necessary to do for the present, to break the ground."

Whitman wrote at this Primer in the early fifties. And there is evidence that he made brief additions to it from time to time in the ten years that followed. The most of the manuscript notes are scribbled on sheets of various tints improvised from the paper covers used on the unbound copies of the 1855 edition. There is later paper and later handwriting. But the notes were largely written in the rather exciting five years before the war. "That stretch of time after 1855 until 1861 was crowded with personal as well as political preparations for war." But after he had issued the first edition of *Leaves of Grass,* and after he found the book surviving into the 1856 and 1860 editions, some of his old plans, this lecture scheme among them, were abandoned. The Primer was thenceforth, as a distinct project, held in abeyance. I remember that in the late eighties he said to me: "I may yet bring the Primer out." And when I laughed incredulously he added: "Well, I guess you are right to laugh: I suppose I never shall. And the best of the Primer stuff has no doubt leaked into my other work." It is indeed true that Whitman gave expression to the substance of the Primer in one way or another. Even some of its sentences are utilized here and there in his prose and verse volumes.

In referring to the Primer upon another occasion, Whitman said: "This subject of language interests me — interests me: I never quite get it out of my mind. I sometimes think the Leaves is only a language experiment — that it is an attempt to give the spirit, the body, the man, new words, new potentialities of speech — an American, a cosmopolitan (the best of America is the best cosmopolitanism) range of self-expression. The new world, the new times, the new peoples, the new vista, need a tongue according — yes, what is more, will have such a tongue — will not be satisfied until it is evolved." But the study brought to bear upon the subject in the manuscript now under view was never resumed. The Primer, therefore, is, as a part of Whitman's serious literary product, of marked significance. Whitman said of it: "It was first intended for a lecture: then when I gave up the idea of lecturing it was intended for a book: now, as it stands, it is neither a lecture nor a book."

As an alternate to his adopted headline I find this among Whitman's memoranda: "The Primer of Words: For American Young Men and Women, For Literati, Orators, Teachers, Musicians, Judges, Presidents, &c."

I have followed the original manuscript without any departures whatever. All its peculiarities of capitalization and punctuation are allowed to remain untouched.

HORACE TRAUBEL.

3440. The heading, from the title through these eight lines, appears only in the facsimile page preceding the text in the published version.

whirled like chain–shot — rocks, defiance, compulsion, houses, iron, locomotives, xx the oak, the pine, the keen eye, the hairy breast, the Texan
ranger, the Boston truckman, the ~~la~~ woman that arouses ~~an~~ man, the man
that arouses a woman. —
The nigger dialect furnishes hundreds of outre ~~names~~ words, many of them
    adopted into the common speech of the mass of the people. —
    ~~Many of~~ Curiously these words show the old English instinct for ~~wide-
open musical and~~ wide open pronunciations as ~~yaller~~ yallah, for yellow —
massah for master — and for rounding off all the corners of words ~~without~~.
The nigger dialect ~~gives~~ has hints of the future ~~musical~~ theory of the modification of all the words of the English language, for musical purposes, for
a native grand opera in America.[3441]

[1]

~~Our~~ Language. —[3442]

  ~~Words are the~~ Much is said of what is spiritual, and of spirituality, in
this, that, ~~and~~ or the other – in objects, expressions. — For me, I see ~~nothing
that exists~~ no object, no expression, no animal, no tree, no art, no book, but
I see, from morning to night, and from night to morning, the spiritual. —
Bodies are all spiritual. — All words are spiritual — nothing is more spiritual
than words. — Whence are they? ~~through~~ along how many thousands and
tens ~~and hundreds~~ of thousands of years have they come? those eluding,
fluid, beautiful, fleshless, realities, Mother, Father, Water, Earth, Me, This,
Soul, Tongue, House, Fire,

———

[2]

      ? outset of Language[3443]

  A great observation will detect ~~sometnes~~ sameness through all languages,
however old, however new, however polished, however rude. — As humanity
is one, under ~~all~~ its amazing diversities, ~~so~~ language is one under its. — The
~~common~~ flippant, ~~observer,~~ reading ~~or studying of~~ on some long–past age,

[3]

wonders at its dead costumes, its amusements, &c.; but the master, ~~below
those animal growths, acknowledges~~ understands well the old, ever–new,
ever–common grounds, below those animal growths. — ~~The master, I say,~~

3441. All of this material, from the heading on, is not in the published version, which
begins with the words, "Much is said . . ."
3442. This heading is omitted in the published version.
3443. Heading omitted in the published version.

Voices

The Americans are goig to be the most fluent and melodious voiced people in the world — and the most perfect users of words. — Words follow Character

nativity,
independence
individuality

~~beholds~~ & between any two ages, any two languages and two humanities, however wide [apart?] in Time & Space   marks well not the superficial shades of difference, but the mass–shades, of a ~~common~~ joint nature. —

[4]   [Drawing of spine on verso]
Our Language.[3444]
    In a little while, ~~here~~ in the United States, ~~this~~ the English Language ~~by far the noblest known~~, enriched ~~with all the~~ with contributions ✕ from all other languages, old and new, will be spoken by ~~more people in American than any other one language any where else is, or probably ever was spoken~~ a hundred millions of people: —

---

~~now~~ perhaps a hundred thousand words ("seventy or eighty thousand words" Noah Webster (of the English language)

[5]
                    Voices[3445]
    The Americans are going to be the most fluent and melodious voiced people in the world – and the most perfect users of words. — Words follow character
            nativity
            independence
            individuality

[6]
    I see that the time is nigh when the ~~shallow~~ etiquette of foreign saloons ~~shall not~~ is to be ~~applied to~~ discharged from this great thing, the renovated English speech in America. — The occasions of the English speech in America are immense, profound, stretch over ten thousand vast cities, over millions of miles of meadows, farms, mountains, men, through thousands of years — the occasions of saloons are for a coterie, ~~for an~~ a bon soir or two, – ~~and~~ involve be~~sides they have~~ waiters standing behind chairs, ⋏ silent, obedient, with bend backs that can bend ⋏ and must often bend. ⋏ ~~How long do you suppose~~

[7]
    What beauty there is in words! What a lurking curious charm in the sound of some words! — ~~Two or three~~ Then voices! Five or six times in a

3444.  Heading omitted in the published version.
3445.  Heading omitted in the published version.

lifetime, (perhaps not so often,) ~~voices~~ you have heard ~~such~~ from men and women ~~speak in such~~ ~~towering~~ such ~~perfect~~ voices, as they spoke the most common word! — What can it be that from ~~such~~ those few men and women made so much out of the most common word!

[8]

Geography, ~~and~~ shipping, steam, the mint, the electric telegraph, rail-roads, and x so forth, have many strong and beautiful words

[9]

mines – iron works – the sugar plantations of Louisiana – the ~~rice~~ cotton crops and the rice crop – ~~wheat~~, Illinois wheat — Ohio corn and pork — Maine lumber – all these sprout in hundreds and hundreds of words, ~~of~~ all tangible and clean–lined, all having texture and beauty.

[10]

To All ~~the~~ thoughts of ~~the~~ your or any one's mind – to all ~~your~~ yearnings, passions, love, hate, ennui, madness, desperation of men for women, and of women for men, — to all ~~our that xx~~ charge~~s~~ and surcharg~~ing~~ ~~that~~ that head ~~that~~ which poises itself on your neck – ~~that~~ & is electric in ~~and that~~ the body beneath your head, ~~and –~~ ~~that~~ or runs with ~~your~~ the blood through your veins – ~~that is~~ or in ~~that~~ those curious incredible miracle[s] ~~called~~ you call ~~your~~ eyesight & hearing – to all these, and the like of these, have been made words. — Such are the words that are never new and never old. —[3446]

[11]

What a history is folded, ~~and folded~~, folded ~~in and in~~ inward and inward again, in the single word I. —

[12]

The words of the Body! – The words of Parentage! The words of ~~Offsp~~ Husband and Wife! – The words of Offspring! The word Mother! – The word Father!

[13]

The words of ~~Manners~~ Behaviour are quite numerous. — They follow the law; they are courteous, grave, have polish, have an ~~odor~~ sound of

3446. Here, and at the ends of other paragraphs, Whitman's dashes have been omitted in the published version, despite Traubel's final statement in his Foreword. In a few other places, too trivial to note, however, Traubel has not followed Whitman's punctuation and paragraphing.

presence, and ~~can easily shame~~ abash all furniture and shallowness out of their sight.

~~Womanly~~ The words of Maternity are all the words that ~~were are~~ were ever spoken by the mouth~~es~~ of ~~man~~ man, the ~~children~~ child of woman – but ⚹ they are reborn words, and the ~~voice~~ mouth of the full-sized mother, daughter, wife, amie, ~~is are~~ does ~~not~~ not ~~hurt~~ offend by using any one [of] them.

[14]

Medicine has hundreds of useful and characteristic words – new means of cure – new schools of doctors – the wonderful anatomy of the body – the names of a thousand diseases – surgeon's terms – hydropathy – all that relates to the great organs of the body. — Medicine The Medical art is always grand — nothing affords a nobler scope for ~~the~~ superior men and women. — It, ~~will~~ of course, will ~~continue~~ never cease to be near ~~and~~ to man, and ~~ce~~ add new terms

[15]

Law, (Medicine), Religion, the Army, the personnel of the Army and Navy, the Arts, stand on their old stock of words, without increase. — In the law, ~~are it~~ is to be noticed a growing impatience with ~~the~~ formulas, and ~~the~~ with diffuseness, and venerable slang. — The personnel of the Army and Navy exists in America, apart from the throbbing life of America – ~~exiles~~ an exile in the land, ⅄ ~~When~~ foreign to the instincts and tastes of the people, and, of course, soon in due time to ~~be~~ give place to something ~~for~~ native, ~~and that has an an of~~ something warmed with the throbs of our own life

[16]

These States are rapidly supplying themselves with new words, called for by new occasions, new facts, new politics, new combinations. — ~~Still furth~~ Far plentier ~~words~~ additions ~~are needed~~ will be needed, and, of course, will be supplied. —

[17]

(Because it is a truth that) the words continually used among the people are, in numberless cases, not the words used in writing, or recorded in the dictionaries by authority. — ~~Probably~~ There are ~~just as~~ many words in daily use, not inscribed in ~~any~~ the dictionary, and seldom or never in any print, ~~as there are words recorded.~~ — Alas, the forms of grammar are ~~seldom — or~~ never ~~ob-~~persistently obeyed, and cannot be. —

The ~~Prop~~ Real Dictionary will give all words that exist in use, the bad words as well as

[18]

any. — The Real Grammar will be that which declares itself a nucleus ~~on~~ of the spirit of the laws, with ~~perfect~~ liberty to all to carry out the the spirit of the laws, even by violating them, if necessary. — The English Language is grandly lawless like the ℀ race who use it. — Or Perhaps – or rather breaks out of the little ? laws to enter truly the higher ones It is so instinct with that which underlies laws, ~~that~~ and the purports of laws, ~~that I think~~ it ~~goes toward the destinati~~ refuses all petty interrup~~t~~uptions in its way ~~toward~~ purports. —

[19]

   <u>Books</u> themselves have their peculiar words — ~~all words,~~ — namely those that are never used ~~except in books~~ in living speech, in the real world, but only used in the worlds of books. — Nobody ever actually talks as books and plays talk

[20]

   ~~Day~~ The Morning has its words, and ~~Night~~ the Evening its words. — How much there is in the word Light! ~~How~~ How vast, surrounding, falling sleeping, noiseless, is the word Night! – It hugs ~~is a word that one a man~~ with ~~welcome, vast,~~ unfelt yet living arms. —

[21]

   Character makes words. — The English stock, ~~natural, fibred, animal,~~ friendly, full of   [?] faults, but fond of women, ~~honest,~~ averse to all folderol, equable, instinctual, just, ~~always never divested of~~ latent with pride and melancholy, ready ~~never~~ with ~~the strong sh~~ brawned arms, with free speech, with the knife–blade for tyrants and the reached hand for slaves, — have put all these in words. — We have them in America, — they are the body of the whole of the past. — We are to justify our inheritance — we ~~too~~ are to pass it on to those who are to còme after us, a thousand years hence, ~~and~~ as we have grown out of the English of a thousand years ago. —

[22]

   American geography, — the plenteousness ~~of~~ and variety of the great nations of the Union – the thousands of settlements – the seacoast – the Canadian north – the Mexican south – California and Oregon – the inland seas – the mountains – Arizona – the prairies – the immense rivers – the

[23]

Many of the slang words among fighting men, gamblers, thieves, prostitutes, are powerful words

~~Many of~~ These words ought to be collected – the bad words as well as the good; — Many of these bad words are fine. ~~specimens~~

[24]
Music has many good words, now technical, but of such rich and ~~fluen~~ juicy character, that they ought to be ~~made~~ taken for common use in writing and speaking. —

[25]
~~All~~ New forms of science, ~~all~~ newer freer characters, may have something in them to need new words. — ~~The~~ One beauty of words is exactitude: — To me, each word out of the        that now compose the English language, has its own meaning, and does not stand for any thing but itself – and there are no two words ~~that are~~ the same ~~and~~ any more than there are two persons the same. —

[26]
Names of characteristic amusements and games,
(Much of America is shown in its newspaper names, and in the names of
        its steamboats, ships,

[27]
What do you think words are? Do you think words are ~~arbitrary~~ positive and original things in themselves? — No: Words are not original and arbitrary in themselves. — Words are ~~a~~ result – they are the progeny of what has been or is in vogue. — If iron

[28]
architecture comes in vogue, as it seems to be coming, words are wanted to ~~express~~ stand for ~~those iron girders, facades~~ all about iron architecture, for the work it causes, for the different branches of work and of the workmen – those blocks of ~~bu te os~~ buildings, seven stories high, with light strong facades, and girders that will not crumble a mite in a thousand years.

[29]
Also words to describe all American peculiarities, ~~and~~ – the splendid and rugged characters that are ~~growing up~~ forming among these states, ~~and have~~ or are already formed, — in the cities, the ~~New York~~ firemen of Mannahatta, and the the target excursionist, and Bowery boy – the Boston truck man – the Philadelphia – ~~the~~
[30]
In America an immense number of new words are needed, ~~fro~~ to embody

the new political facts, the compact of the Declaration of Independence, and of the Constitution – the union of the States – the new–States – the Congress – the modes of election – the stump speech – the

[31]

ways of electioneering – addressing the people – ~~Clothing~~ stating all that is to be said in ~~such~~ modes ~~th~~ that fit the life and experience of the Indianian, the Michiganian, the Vermonter, the men of Maine, ~~m~~ the

[32]

– also words to answer the ~~grea~~ modern ~~faith,~~ rapidly spreading, faith, of the vital equality of women with men, ~~and of those then~~ and that they are to be placed on ~~the same grounds,~~ an exact plane, politically, socially, and in business, ~~as~~ with men.

[33]

   Words are wanted to supply the copious trains of ~~facts~~ facts, and flanges of facts, feelings, arguments, and adjectival facts, growing out of all new ~~sciences~~ knowledges, Phrenology.

[34]

   Drinking brandy, ~~or~~ gin, beer, is generally fatal to the perfection of the voice; – ~~A~~ Meanness of mind, ~~and all is~~ the same; — Gluttony, in eating, of course the same; a thinned habit of body, or a rank habit of body – mastur- bation, inordinate going with women, ~~total and spoil sternly~~ rot the voice. — Yet ~~none~~ no man can have a great vocalism, ~~whose amiab~~ who has no ex- perience of ~~love~~ woman who with woman and no who has no experience with man. – The ~~voice is rich with the exp arousing with~~ final fibre and ~~xxxxx~~ charm of the voice, follows the chaste ~~experience~~ drench of love.

[35]

   The great Italian singers are above all others in the world,/ ~~for reasons precisely sim like the reasons quite or for~~ from causes quite the same as those that make the voices of the ~~New strong~~ native healthy substrata of ~~New York~~ Mannahatta young men, especially the drivers of horses, and all whose work leads to free loud calling and commanding, ~~the pos~~ have such a ring and freshness. —

[36]

   Pronunciation of Yankees is nasal ~~and chromatic – it is~~ and offensive – it has ~~flat~~ the flat tones. It could probably be ~~remedied entirely~~ changed by placing only those teachers in schools who have rich ripe voices – and by the children practising ~~the~~ to speak from the chest and in the gutteral ? and baritone ? ~~pitch of~~ methods voice. — All sorts of physical, moral and mental deformities are inevitably returned in the voice. —

[37]

| | |
|---|---|
| robust | stern |
| brawny | resistance |
| athletic | bracing |
| muscular | rude |
| acrid | rugged |
| harsh | rough |
| rugged | shaggy |
| severe | bearded |
| pluck | arrogant |
| grit | haughty[3447] |
| effrontery | |

The ~~nations~~ races that in their realities are supple, obedient, cringing have hundreds of words to express hundreds of forms of acts, thoughts, flanges, of those ~~ideas~~ realities, which the English tongue knows nothing of

The English tongue is full of strong words native or adopted to express the blood–born passion of the ~~Teutonic~~ race for rudeness and resistance, as against ~~the~~ polish and all acts to give in:

These ~~are~~ words are alive and sinewy, — they walk, look, step with an air of ~~danger~~ command. — They will ~~always~~ often ~~sw~~ lead [the] rest – they will not follow – How can they follow? They will appear        [?]

[38]

English words. — Even people's names were spelt ~~in~~ by themselves, sometimes one way sometimes another. — Public necessity remedies all troubles. — Now, in the 80th year of These States, there is a little diversity in the ways of spelling words, and ~~great~~ much diversity in the ways of pronouncing them; — ~~but~~ steamships, railroads, newspapers, submarine telegraphs, will probably bring them in. — If not, it is not important. —

[39]

So in the accents and inflections of words. — ~~The core coherence~~ Language must cohure – it cannot be left loosely to float ~~or~~ – to fly away. — Yet

---

3447. This list of words does not appear this way in the published version, but is in narrative style, separated by commas, after "all acts to give in:" in the next paragraph.

all the ~~laws~~ rules of the accents and inflections of words drop before a perfect voice – ~~it~~ that may follow the rules, or be ignorant of them – it is indifferent which. — Pronunciation is the ~~one~~ stamina of language – it is language. — ⚹ The noblest pronunciation, in a city or race, marks ~~a~~ the noblest city or race, or ~~the~~ descendents ⚹ thereof. –

[40]

Why are words names so mighty? – Because ~~faiths~~ facts, ancestry, maternity, ~~is~~ faiths, are. — Slowly, sternly, inevitably, move the souls of the earth. — ~~All is inextrikable from precedents, and therefore should be~~ so. — and words names are its their signs

[41]

Kosmos–words, Words of the ~~Enlargement~~ Free Expansion of Thought, History, Chronology, Literature, // ~~Kosmos words,~~ are ~~becoming~~ showing themselves, with ~~grand large and~~ foreheads muscular necks and breasts. — ~~The~~ These gladden me! — I put my arms around them – touch my lips to them. — The past ~~is calm ten thousand years~~ hundred centuries have confided much to me, ~~but~~ yet they mock me, ~~and~~ frowning. — ~~I cannot tell~~ I think I am ~~startled at~~ done with many of the words of the past hundred centuries. — I am ~~terrified~~ mad that their poems, bibles, words, ~~yet represent~~ still rule and represent the earth, and are not ~~at all yet overlaid~~. — superceded. ~~"Walt Whitman, are will you be impatient?~~ But why do I say so? — I ~~w~~ must not, — will not, be impatient. —

[42]

~~Why shou~~ In ~~these~~ American city excursions, for military practice, for firing at the target, for all the exercises of health and manhood – why should not women accompany them? — ~~Though those states,~~ I expect to see ~~the day,~~ ~~or time~~ the time in ~~those in~~ Politics, Business, Public ~~Conventions~~ Gatherings, Processions, Excitements, when women shall not be divided from men, but shall take their part ~~in~~ on the same terms as men. ~~take their part. only then~~ ~~What were men being fitter to stand back those men that~~ What sort of women have ~~xxxx through These States~~ Massachusetts, Ohio, Virginia, Pennsylvania, and the rest, ~~to~~ correspondent with ~~what~~ what they continually want? Sometimes I ~~th~~ have fancied that only from superior hardy women ~~are to~~ can rise the future superiorities of These States.

[43]

⟨gallus³⁴⁴⁸ Man's words, for the Young men of these states, are all words that

---

3448. Omitted in the published version.

have arisen out of the qualities of mastership, ~~freedom go~~ going first, brunt-
ing danger first, — words to identify ~~an erect a ma an athletic~~ a hardy ⚹
~~upright~~ boyhood — ~~an unstained~~ knowledge – an ~~sweet~~ erect, sweet lusty,
body, without taint ~~those where whence all~~ choice and clear of its ~~love life~~
pure power —

[44]

The spelling of words is subordinate. — ~~To Great Excessive nicety~~ Mor-
bidness ~~about~~ for nice spelling, ~~me~~ and tenacity for or against some one
letter or so, means dandyism and impotence in literature. — Of course the
great writers must have digested all these things, — ~~and~~ passed lexicons, etymologies, ~~ayntapes,~~ orthographies, through ~~him~~ them. — and extracted ~~only~~
the nutriment. Modern taste is for ~~bref~~ brevity and for ranging ~~in~~ words in
spelling–classes; – Probably, the words of the English tongue can never be
ranged in spelling–classes. — The Phonetic ? Spelling is on natural principles – it has arbitrary forms of letters, ~~for all~~ and combinations of letters,
for all sounds. — : It may ~~owe~~ in time prevail – it surely will prevail if it is
~~xxxxxxx~~ best it should. — ~~For a long will while after~~ For many hundred
years there was nothing like ~~uniform~~ settled spelling in ~~the~~ most

[45]

A perfect user of words uses things – ~~they~~ they exude Ȧ ~~po~~ in power and
beauty from him – miracles from his hands – miracles from his mouth –
                    [?]        [?]
~~things,~~ lilies, clouds, sunshine, woman, poured consciously – things, whirled
like chain–shot – rocks, defiance, compulsion, houses, iron, locomotives, ~~a~~ the
oak, the pine, the keen eye, the hairy breast, the Texan ranger, the Boston
truckman, the ~~la~~ woman that arouses a man, the man that arouses a
woman. —

[46]

Tavern words, such as have reference to drinking, or the compliments of
    those who drink – the names of some ~~two~~ three hundred different Ameri-
    can tavern–drinks in one part or another of these states. —

[47]

Words of all degrees of dislike, from just a tinge, onward ~~to the and~~ or
    deepward. —
Words of approval, admiration, friendship. (~~It is to be~~ This is to be said
    among the young men of these states, that with a wonderful tenacity of
    friendship, and ~~a manliness of~~ passionate fondness for their friends, and
    always a manly readiness to make friends, they yet have remarkably

few words, ~~to~~ of names for the friendly sentiments. — They seem to be words that do not thrive here among the ~~mse~~ muscular classes, where the real quality of friendship is always freely to be found. — Also they are

[48]

words which the muscular classes, ~~and~~ the young men of these states, ~~are~~ rarely use, and have an aversion for; — they never give words to their most ardent friendships. —

[49]

Words of politics are numerous in these states, and many of them peculiar. — The western states have terms of their own
Words of Costune[3449]

[50]

— ~~the all new goods~~ the Presidents message – the political meeting – the committees – the resolutions —
— new vegetables — new trees — new animals ~~succeed and breed,~~
If success and breed follow the camels and dromedaries, that have are now just introduced into Texas, to ~~b be used~~ be used for travel and traffic over the —[?]— vast wilds between the lower Mississippi and the Pacific, ~~an immense~~ a number of new words will have to be tried after them.

[51]

Politics
      (bring in last of "Appeal"

Words of Epithets. — [3450]

~~American speech and writing demo~~ The ~~tastes~~ appetite of the people of These States in ~~public~~ popular speeches and writings, ~~are~~ is for ~~great~~ unhemmed lattitude, coarseness, directness, live epithets, explitives, words of opprobium, resistance. — ~~in public speeches and writings.~~ — This I understand because I have the ~~same~~ taste myself, — ~~I have pleasure in the use, on fit occasions,~~ as large as largely as any —[?]— one, of

| traitor | mean curse |
| coward | backslider |

3449. Omitted in the published version.
3450. These three lines are omitted in the published version.

| | |
|---|---|
| liar | thief |
| shyster | impotent |
| skulk | lickspittle[3451] |
| doughface | |
| trickster | |

[52]

~~As long as~~ Appendant, I see,  The great writers, ~~I see,~~ are often select of their audiences. — The greatest writers ~~are~~ only ~~they who~~ are ~~perfectly at~~ well-pleased and at their ease among the ~~commonalty,~~ unlearned ~~and create so whom all~~ are received by ~~unlea~~ common men and women ~~receive as~~ familiarly, ~~and who~~ do not ~~puzzle~~ hold out obscure, ~~and~~ but ~~are~~ come welcome ~~at~~ to table, bed, leisure, by day and night. —

[53]

A perfect writer ~~will~~ would make words  ~~do any thing that any thing can do~~ sing, dance, kiss, ~~copulate~~ do the male and female act, bear children, weep, bleed, rage, stab, steal, ~~sw~~ fire cannon, steer ships, ~~play overtures of music perform operas,~~ sack cities, ~~shoot trot on h~~ charge with cavalry ~~or artillery~~ or infantry, or do any thing that ~~any thing~~ man or woman or the natural powers can do.

[54]

Latent, in a great ~~writer,~~ user of words, must actually be all passions, crimes, trades, animals, stars, God, sex, the past, night, space, metals, and the like – because these are the words, and ~~if~~ he who is not these, plays with a foreign tongue, ~~talking xxx~~ turning helplessly to dictionaries and authorities. How can I tell you? — ~~I dare say I cannot tell you, after all.~~ — I ~~only~~ put many things ~~now~~ on record that you will not understand at first – perhaps not in a year – but they must be are to be understood. — ~~I see~~ The earth, I see, writes with prodigal clear hands all summer, forever, and all winter also, content and certain to be understood/# in time. —

[55]

as, doubtless, only the greatest ~~poet~~ user of words himself ~~ever~~ fully enjoys and understands himself

---

3451.  Like the previous list, this one is arranged in narrative style, separated by commas, in the published version.

[56]

(Mannahatta[3452]

Words of Names of Places, ~~give a make a~~ are strong, ~~and~~ copious, ~~unshaped untrimmed~~ unruly ~~ingredient~~ in the repertoire ~~of~~ for ~~our the~~ American pens and tongues. — The Names of These States — the names of Counties, Cities, Rivers, Mountains, Villages, Neighborhoods — ~~Some~~ poured plentifully from ~~the~~ each of the ~~va~~ languages that ~~have contributed~~ graft ~~to~~ the English language – or named from some ~~naturally~~ peculiarity of water or earth, or ~~from~~ some event that happened there – often ~~rudely~~ named, from death, from some animal, from some of those subtle analog/ies that the ~~ages, peo~~ common people are so quick to perceive. — The names

[57]

in the list of the Post Offices of these States are ~~a~~ studies. — ~~They few will realize they indicate~~

What name a city has – What name a State, ~~a~~ river, sea, mountain, wood, ~~mea~~ prairie, has – ~~I think it~~ is ~~not~~ no ~~an~~ indifferent matter. — ~~The~~ All aboriginal names ~~are all~~ sound good; ~~I am~~ was asking for something savage and luxuriant, and behold here are the aboriginal names. I see how they are being preserved. The[y] ~~all~~ are honest words – they give the true length, breadth, depth – They all fit, — Mississippi! – ~~how~~ the word ~~rolls,~~ winds with chutes – ~~and~~ it ~~is hides~~ [?] rolls a stream three thousand miles long; — Ohio, ~~the~~ Connecticut, Ottawa, ~~fit this~~ Monongahela, ~~is as true – Ontario~~ ~~Delaware~~ all fit. and

[58]

~~There is~~ Names are ~~wonderful.~~ magic — ~~all words~~ — ~~the~~ one word/ ~~brings up suc opens such~~ can pour such a flood ~~in~~ through the soul. — ~~I have mentioned Christ~~ – To-day I ~~will always~~ will mention Christ's before all other names. — ~~But what heres~~ Grand words of names are still left. — What is it that flows through me at the sight of the word ~~Hermes, or Pythagoras,~~ Socrates, ~~or~~ or Plato, or ~~Pythagoras, or Hermes,~~ or Cincinnatus, or Alfred of the olden time – or at the sight of the word Columbus, or Shakespeare

[59]

~~or Voltaire~~ or Rosseau or Mirabeau – ar at the sight of the ~~words~~ word George Washington, or Jefferson, or R. W. Emerson?

---

3452.   As was Traubel's practice, he omitted this title in the published version.

[60]

Out of Christ are divine words. — <u>Out of this saviour</u>

Some words are ~~divine sweet~~ fresh–smelling lilies roses to the soul, bloom-
ing without failure. — the name of Christ — all ~~Such~~ words ~~are those~~ that
have arisen from the life and ~~and~~ death ~~Christ~~ of ~~Jesus~~ Christ, the ~~saviour
of men, the~~ divine son, ~~of Mary,~~ who ~~was crucified~~ went about speaking
perfect words, no patois – whose life was perfect, – ~~who the well – beloved,
whose hands,~~ the touch of whose hands and feet ~~did~~ was miracles – who was
crucified – his flesh laid in a shroud, in the grave, but

[61]

A few characteristic words       improve this

    Words give us to see   (list of poets – Hindoo – Homer – Shakespeare

      Pythagoras   –   Socrates   –   Christ,
      Plato            Sesostris,      Menes that
      Zoroaster                         walked with
      Menu                              Ammon [ ? ] [3453]

I say that ~~A~~ Say, either liberty is to have the ~~life~~ blood of slavery, or slavery
is to have the blood of liberty. —

[62]

                    ( ? ~~A   Suggestive~~ Primer[3454]

Words of Names of Persons, thus far, ~~follow the are result from the precedents of have no other return as of s~~ still return the ~~other~~ old continents and
races — return the past three thousand years, – perhaps twenty thousand – ~~re-
turn from~~ return the Hebrew Bible, Greece, Rome, France, ~~the Anglo~~ the
Goths, the Celts, Scandinavia, Germany, England. — Still questions come:
What flanges ~~are there appear, wait, forms, to be fo~~ are practicable for names
of persons that ~~expand from ourselves?~~ mean These States? — What ~~are~~ is
there in the best aboriginal names? What ~~are~~ is there in strong words of qualities, bodily, mental, – a name given to the ~~mos~~ cleanest and most beautiful
body, or to the offspring of the same? — What is there that will conform to
the genius of These States, and to all the facts X ? — What escape, ~~without~~

[63]

with perfect freedom, without affectation, ~~is there~~ from the shoals of Johns,
Peters, Davids, Marys,

3453.  In place of this list, in the published version, Traubel has a footnote after "grave"
that reads: "Whitman here inserts a memorandum, a sort of self-query, to this effect: 'A few
characteristic words — words give us to see — (list of poets — Hindoo — Homer — Shakespeare
— Pythagoras, Plato, Zoroaster, Menu, Socrates, Sesostris, Christ). Improve this.' — H. T."
3454.  Omitted in the published version.

Or on what ~~other names~~ happy principle, popular and fluent, ~~shall~~ could other words be prefixed or suffixed to these, to make them show who they are, ~~and~~ what land they were born in, what government, ~~wat S~~ which of The States, ~~and~~ what genius, mark, blood, ~~di~~ times, ~~h~~ have coined them with ~~their own~~ strong–cut coinage?

[64]

The ~~heart~~ subtle charm of beautiful pronunciation is not in dictionaries grammars, marks of accent, ~~or any~~ formulas of a language or ~~any thing in the~~ any laws or rules. —The ~~heart~~ charm of all the beautiful pronunciation of all words, of all tongues, is ~~a~~ in perfect, flexible vocal organs, ~~flexible~~ and in a developed harmonious soul. — ~~These make spe all words A Comm~~ All words, spoken ~~by~~ from these, have ~~superb~~ deeper sweeter sounds, new meanings, impossible on any less terms. — Such meanings, such sounds, continually wait in ~~all words,~~ every word that exists — in these words, — perhaps slumbering, ~~not worked~~ through years, ~~perhaps~~ closed from all ~~easy,~~ tympans of temples, ~~and~~ lips, brains, until ~~the that of~~ that comes which has ~~that~~ the quality ~~of that none wa~~ waiting patiently ~~in~~ in ~~that~~ the words. — ~~and seem~~ [?] ~~never to die.~~ — [3455]

[65]

The blank left by Words wanted, but ~~not yet adopted~~ unsupplied ~~have~~ has sometimes an ~~ghastly~~ unnamably putrid ~~fr most frightful indescribably~~ ~~It is a bitter~~ cadaverous meaning. — It glares is talks arose [?] louder than ~~sounds~~ tongues.

~~What a battl bitter taste is throws~~ What ~~an acrid~~ a ~~rank unsweetened~~ stinging taste is ~~yet~~ left in ~~words, all~~ that literature and or conversation ~~that there are that there have~~ where have not yet been ~~adopted~~ served up, by resistless consent, words ~~that~~ to be freely used in ~~later~~ books, rooms, at table, any where, to specifically mean the act male and female. — ~~What can tell  The~~

[66]

Likely there are other words wanted. — Of ~~all~~ words wanted, the matter is summed up in this; When the time comes for them to represent any thing or any state of things, the words will surely follow. — The lack of any words, I say again, is as historical as the existence of words. As for me, I feel ~~many~~ a hundred realities, ~~perfectly well~~ clearly determined in me, that words are

---

3455.   Although the MS. has a cancellation line, apparently drawn by Whitman, Traubel used in the printed version this material from "The charm of the beautiful pronunciation . . ." to ". . . patiently waiting in the words." And there was no new paragraph until he had come to the end of the sentence whose last words are ". . . act male and female."

not yet formed to represent. — Men like me, // also women, our counter-parts, perfectly equal, will gradually get to be more and more numerous — perhaps swiftly, in shoals; — then the words will also follow, in shoals. — It is the glory and superb rose-bloom hue of the English language, any-where, that it admits of favors growth as the skin does – that it can soon be-come, wherever that is needed, the tough skin of a superior man or woman. —

[67]

The whole art of the great use of words, dwindles into a would be a stain, a smutch, in before but for the stamina of things. —Now

[68]

For in manners, poems, orations, music, friendship, authorship, what is not said is just as important as what is said, and gives as out holds just as much meaning. —

fond of men, as a living woman is — fond of women, as a living man is.

[69]

I like a limber, lashing tongue: — fierce words — I like it them applied to myself – and I I would like to see it them in newspapers, courts, debates, congress. — The liberty, the brawn of These States – What do Do you sup-pose they the liberty/ies and the brawn of These States have to do only with deli-cate lady–words? with gloved gentleman–words? (?) Bad Presidents, bad judges, bad clients, the bad editors, owners of slaves, and the long ranks of Northern political suckers, monopolists, infidels, (robbers, traitors, suborned,) castrated persons, impotent persons, shaved persons, supplejacks, ecclesiastics, men not fond of women, and women not fond of men, women not will cry down the use of strong, cutting, beautiful rude words – but To the manly instincts of the People it will be different they will forever be welcome. to them. —

[70]

In words of names, the ear mouth and ear of the people prefers love are averse brevity and no show antipathy to titles, or Misters, handles – they love short first names, abbreviated to their mouths, lips: Tom, Bill, Walt, Jack. —These are to enter into literature, and be voted for on political tickets for the great offices. —

[71]

Expletives, Words naming the act male and female. — Words of Curious words and phrases, of assent or inquiry. Nicknames, either to persons or customs. (Many actions  many kinds of character, and many of the fashions of dress have names among two thirds of the people, that would never be understood among the remaining third, and never appear in print.)

[72]
F   Factories, mills, and all the processes of hundreds of different manufactures, grow thousands of words. — Cotton, and woollen, and silk goods – hemp, rope, carpets, paper – hangings, paints, tin roofing preparations, hardware, furniture, paper–mills, the printing–offices with their wonderful improvements, paper engraving, daguerreotyping,

Iron This is the age of the metal Iron. — Iron, and with all that it it does, or that belongs to iron, or flanges from it, has a prolific sent results in words: from the minds mines, a thousand words they have been drawn, as the ore has been drawn. — Following the universal laws of words, these are welded together in hardy forms and characters. — They are ponderous, strong, definite,

[73]
not indebted to the antique — they are iron iron words, wrought and cast. — I consider see them all good, and faithful, trem sturdy, massive, permanent words. — I love well these iron words of 1856. — Coal has its words also, that assimilate very much with those of iron. —

Gold of course has always its words. — The mint, the American coinage the dollar piece, the fifty dollar or one hundred dollar piece — California, the metallic basis of banking, chemical tests of gold — all these have their words. —

[74]
California-words
Canada Words
Yankee Words
Mannahatta Words,
Virginia Words
Caroli
Florida and Alabama Words,
Texas Words
Mexican and Nicaraguan Words,
California Words,
Ohio, Illinois, and Indiana Words,[3456]

3456. This list and the next one are both run in, in narrative style, in the published version.

[75]

The different mechanics have different words – all however ~~following~~ under ~~gr a the~~ a few great over-arching laws. — There are

| | |
|---|---|
| Carpenter's words | Tailor's words |
| Mason's words | Hatter's words, |
| Blacksmith's words | Weaver's words |
| Shoemaker's words | Painter's words, |

~~The modern American printing press~~

~~Farmers~~ The <u>Farmer's words</u> are immense. — They are mostly old, ~~have~~ partake of ripeness, home, the ground, — ~~and~~ have nutriment, like wheat and milk. Farm words are added to, now, by a new class of words, from the introduction of ~~scientific~~ chemistry into farming, and from the introduction of numerous machine~~rys~~ into the barn and field. —

[76]

The nigger dialect furnishes hundreds of outre ~~names~~ words, many of them adopted into the common speech of the mass of people. —

~~Many of~~ Curiously, these words show the old English instinct for ~~wide-open musical and~~ wide open pronunciations, as ~~yaller~~ <u>yallah</u>, for yellow – <u>massah</u> for master – and for rounding off all the corners of words. ~~without~~ The nigger dialect ~~gives~~ has hints of the future ~~musical~~ theory of the modification of all the words of the English language, for musical purposes, for a native grand opera in America

[76.1]
[Horace Traubel's autograph:]     Sheet to Negroes

---

The nigger dialect[3457]

---

[77]

leaving the words just as they are for writing and speaking, but ~~now~~ the same words so modified as to answer perfectly for musical purposes, on grand and simple principles. — Then we should have two sets of words, male and female as they should be, in these states, both equally understood by the people, giving a fit much needed medium to that passion for music, ~~in~~ which is ~~greater stronger~~ deeper and purer in America than in any other land in the world. — ~~and is~~ The music of America [is] to adopt the Italian methods, and expand it to vaster, simpler, far superber effects. — ~~Above — all,~~

3457.  There is no break, only a comma, between "in America" and "leaving the words," in the published version.

~~it~~ It is not to be satisfied till it comprehends the people, and is comprehended by them. —

[78]

Sea–words, coast words, sloop–words, sailor's and boatmen's words, words of ships, are numerous in America. — One fourth of the people of these states are aquatic ~~in character~~ — love the water, love to be near it, smell it, sail on it, swim it in it, fish, clam, trade to and fro upon it. — To be much on the water, ~~and~~ or in constant sight of it, affects words, ~~affects character,~~ the voice, the passions. — Around the markets, among the fish–smacks, along the wharves, you hear a thousand ~~strong a never~~ – words, never yet printed in the repertoire of ~~no~~ any lexicon, — words ~~that are to the life of strong~~ strong words solid as ~~timber timbers,~~ logs, and ~~of~~ more beauty to me than any of the antique. —

[78.1–14]

[Horace Traubel autograph:] This is insert #1 (see page 467 Atlantic pages). [Printed page on *The Gospel of Freedom,* a forthcoming book, by Mowry Saben, United Publishing House, 173 Purchase Street, New Bedford, Mass. Another sheet with Horace Traubel autograph:] I have followed the original manuscript without any departures whatever. All its peculiarities of capitalization & punctuation are allowed to remain untouched. [Then follows pages 460–470 of *The Atlantic Monthly,* 1904, containing Walt Whitman's "An American Primer," with a prefatory note by Horace Traubel; these clipped pages have numerous minor MS changes, made by Traubel, as they have apparently been used to set the book publication of *An American Primer* (Boston: Small, Maynard & Company, 1904).]

[79]

Words of ~~all~~ the Laws of the Earth,[3458]
Words of the Stars, and about them,
Words of the Sun and Moon,
Words of Geology, ~~Chemistry Gegro~~ History, Geography,
Words of Ancient Races,
Words of ~~Me~~ the Medieval Races,
Words of the Progress of ~~Law~~, Religion, Law, Art, Government,
Words of the ~~Topography~~ surface of the Earth, grass, rocks, trees, flowers, grains, and the like,

---

3458. All of this material, in these lists, through the line ending "Repugnance and the like," is printed in the published version the way Whitman wrote it.

Words of Climates,
Words of the Air and Heavens,
Words of the Birds of the air, and of insects,
Words of Animals,

[80]

Words of ~~the~~ Men and Women — the hundreds of different nations,
    tribes, colors, and other distinctions,
Words of the Sea
Words of Modern Leading Ideas,
Words of Modern Inventions, Discoveries, engrossing Themes, Pursuits,
Words of ~~the~~ These States — the Revolutionary Year 1, Washington, the
    Primal Compact, the Second Compact, (namely the Constitution) –
    ~~the~~ – trades, farms, wild lands, iron, steam, slavery, elections, Cali-
    fornia, and so forth,
Words of ~~all~~ the Body, Senses, Limbs, Surface, Interior,

[81]

Words of dishes to eat, or of naturally produced things to eat,
Words of clothes,
Words of implements,
Words of furniture
Words of all kinds of Building and Constructing,
Words of Human Physiology
Words of ~~Phren~~ Human Phrenology,
Words of Music,
Words of Feebleness, Nausea, Sickness, Ennui, Repugnance, and the like,

[82]

> (One single name belongs to one single
> place only – as ~~a word a~~ a key–word of
> ~~a X book~~ may be best used only once
> in the book.

In most instances A characteristic word once used in a poem, speech, or
what not, is then exhausted; ~~H~~ he who thinks he is going to produce effects
by ~~piling~~ freely using strong words, is ~~but a~~ ignorant of words. —[3459] A ~~great~~
true composition in words, ~~is~~ returns the human body, male or female —
that is the most perfect composition, and shall be best–beloved by men and

---

3459. Traubel, in the published version, here inserts the sentence beginning, "One
single name belongs."

women, and shall last the longest, which slights no part of the body, and repeats no part of the body. — To make a ~~good great~~ perfect composition in words is more than to make the best building or machine, or ~~any~~ the best statue, or picture. — It ~~is~~ – shall be the glory of the greatest masters to make ~~a~~ perfect compositions in words. —

[83]

As wonderful delineations of character – as     as the picturesque of men, women, history –     as     these (plays of Shakespeare & the rest are grand – our obligations to them are incalculable ~~It~~ Other facts remains to be considered – their foreignness to us in much of their spirit – the sentiment under which they were written, that caste is not to be questioned – that the *ty* ~~kind~~, [?] ~~the~~ nobleman is of one blood, and the —

[84]

Costumes ~~refer~~ are retrospective, — they ~~refer to~~ rise out of the substrata of ~~the~~ education, equality, ignorance, caste, and the like.

~~The day is soon to~~ A nation that imports its costumes, imports deformity. — ~~An individual that~~ I see that the day is to come very soon in America when there will not be ~~on~~ a flat level of costumes,

~~A man that is~~ Shall one man be afraid, or ~~a~~ one woman ~~that~~ be ~~is~~ afraid to dress in a beautiful, ~~and~~ decorous, natural, wholesome, inexpensive manner, because many ~~thousands hundreds~~ thousands dress ~~preposterously~~? in the reverse manner? ~~or because Now~~ There is this also, I see, ~~this~~ about costumes – ~~thousands of~~ many ~~keep~~ save themselves from being exiles, and keep each other in countenance by being alike foolish, dapper, extravagant[3460]

[85]

(add to other —)

~~For~~ Probably there is this truth to be said about the Anglo–Saxon breed that ~~it has~~ in real vocal use it has less ~~us~~ of the words of the various phases of friendship and love than any other race, and more friendship and love. — ~~Our~~ The literature, so full of love, is ~~a~~ begotten ~~succession of the~~

[86]

An American Primer.[3461]

---

begetting of the old ~~court~~ Celtic metrical romances, and of the extravagant

3460. Though cancelled by Whitman, this sentence was used by Traubel in the published version.

3461. Not meant to be printed, this was omitted in the published version.

lays of those who sang and narrated, in France, and thence in England ~~Ireland,~~ — and of Italian extravaganzas — and all that sighing, vowing, kissing, dying, that was in songs in European literature, in the sixteenth century. — Still, it seems as if this love–sickness ~~of~~ engrafted on our literature were only a fair response and enjoyment ~~to after conn~~ [?] ~~the a~~ that people nourish themselves with, after repressing ~~th in~~ their· words. —

[87]
   The Americans, like the English, probably make love worse than any other race. —

[88]
                    Voices.
These follow character, ⫽ and ~~Vocalism is~~ nothing is better than a superb
        vocalism.[3462]
~~Openness,~~
~~What a charm there is in~~
~~Would you be well beloved?~~ –
[Paper turned over, and started anew:]
   I think this land is ~~co~~ covered with/the weeds and chaff of literature.

[89]
        Names
_____

California is sown thick with the names of all the little and big saints
        — (Chase them away and substitute aboriginal names

[90]
   What is the ~~strange charm~~ fitness — ~~our~~ – What the ~~fitness~~ strange charm
of aboriginal names? — Monongahela   (rep) – it rolls with venison richness
upon the palate

[91]
Among names to be Revolutionised that of the City of
                    "Baltimore." —

[92]
   Never will I Allude to the English Language or tongue ~~with~~ without

_____

   3462. This sentence, following the words, ". . . any other race. — " reads in the published version — with no new paragraph — as follows: "Voices follow character, and nothing is better than a superb vocalism." The last sentence in the paragraph begins, "I think this land . . ."

~~gratitude deference, appreciation~~ exultation ~~and p̶h̶r̶aise~~ — This is the tongue ~~It It~~ that spurns laws, as ~~language~~ the greatest tongue must. It is ~~surely~~ the ~~most capacious of all tongues~~ vital ~~yet language Ten~~ tongue // . ~~an greater than all the rest.~~ — — of all — full of ease, definiteness and power, — full of sustenance. — An enormous treasure–house, ~~and~~ or range of treasure houses, arsenals, granary, ~~stocked all~~ chock ~~up~~ full with so many contributions ~~wrested~~ from the north and from the south, from Scandinavia, from Greece ~~.~~ and Rome ~~,~~ — From ~~the~~ Spaniards, Italians, and the French – that its own sturdy home–dated Angles ~~roots~~ bred words ~~have~~ have long been outnumbered by the foreigners, – whom they lead — which is all good, enough, ~~as it should~~ and indeed must be. —

[93]
America owes immeasurable respect and love to the past, and to ~~the an~~ many ancestries, for many inheritances – but of all that America ~~owes~~ has rec'd ~~to~~ from the past, ~~to~~ from the mothers and fathers of laws, arts, letters, &c. by far the greatest inheritance is the English Language — so long in growing — so fitted

[94]
### American Names[3463]
All the greatness of any land, ~~lies~~ at any time, lies folded in its names. — ~~Think~~ Would ~~you~~ I recall ~~upon up any~~ some particular country or age, ~~the greatest~~,? the most ancient?  the greatest? — I ~~call~~ recall a few names, — a mountain, or ~~(cha~~ 'sierra of mountains — a sea or bay — a river, — some mighty city — some deed of persons, friends or enemies — some event, perhaps a great war, perhaps a greater peace; — some ~~sage era lan era~~ time-marking and ~~land~~ place–marking ~~teacher, inventor~~ philosoph, divine person, king, bard, goddess

[95]
captain, discoverer, or the like. — Thus does history, in all things, hang around a few names. — Thus does all human interest hang around names. —

[96]
~~It is a problem~~ All men experience it – but no man ciphers it out.
What is the curious rapport of names? — ~~No man knows. — can tell fo~~r
I have been informed that no man has ~~ever sxxxxxed there~~ there are ~~persons~~ people who say ~~that~~ it is not important about names, ~~or words~~ – one word

3463.  Omitted in the published version: *American Names.*

is as good as another, ~~as long as~~ if the designation ~~is generally passes and in is generally is~~ be understood. — I say that nothing is more important than names. — ~~All language~~ is ~~only nomenclature~~ Is art important? — ~~Are~~ Are forms? ~~forms shapes important? — Is art?~~ Great clusters of nomenclature, is a land, include

[97]
Needed in American Nomenclature[3464]
Appropriate names for the Months — (Those now used perpetuate old myths
Appropriate names for the Days of the Week (Those now used xxx per-
    petuate Teutonic and Greek x divinities)
Appropriate names for Persons American men, women, & children (Those
    now
Appropriate names for American places, cities, Rivers, counties &c — The
    word county itself should be changed

Names of streets[3465]
Numbering the streets, as a general thing, with a few irresistible exceptions,
    is very good. —

[98]
~~I say that~~
    ~~The native names of any country are its~~
    No country can have its own poems without it have its own names. —
    The ~~River~~ name of Niagara should be substituted for the St Lawrence
~~should be changed —~~

[99]
Among the places that stand in need of fresh appropriate names are the
    great cities of St. Louis, New Orleans, St Pauls'
    — and in the interior of this State, the beautiful cities of Rome (Syra-
    cuse,) it already has already a perfectly ⱥⱥ sound and appropriate name,
    namely Salina[3466]

[100]
The whole theory and practice of the naming of College societies must

---

3464. This line and the following ones, through, ". . . should be changed," are all run together as one sentence in the published version.
    3465. These three words omitted in the published version.
    3466. This unfinished sentence, from " — and in the interior" to "namely Salina," is omitted in the published version.

be re–made ~~anew~~, on superior American principles. — ~~which, of course, re-~~ ~~quires that that the~~ The old theory and practice of classical education ~~should~~ is to give way, and a new race of teachers ~~should~~ is to appear. I say we have here, now, a greater age to celebrate, greater ~~though~~ ideas to ~~celebrate and~~ embody than any thing ever in Greece or Rome – or ~~that are~~ in the names of Jupiters, Jevovahs, xxxxx Apollos and their myths. —

[101]

The great proper names used in America must commemorate ~~what dates~~ ~~from~~ things belonging to America, and dating thence. — ~~For~~ Because What is America for? ~~for?~~ ⅄ To commemorate the old myths ~~and goddesses~~ and the gods? ⅄ ~~Or~~ To repeat the Mediterraneanean here? Or the uses and growths of Europe here? — No; — (Nä-o̅-o̅) but to destroy all ~~them~~ those ~~growth~~ from the purposes of ~~mankind~~ the earth, and to erect a new ~~world~~ earth in their place. —

[102]

( <u>All lies folded in names.</u>

( ~~As if we~~

I have heard it said that when the spirit arises that does not ~~subordi-~~ brook submission and imitation, it will throw off ~~all~~ the ultramarine names. — That spirit already walks the streets of the cities of These States — I, ~~stand~~ ~~here an illustr~~ and others, illustrate it. — I say America too ~~must~~ shall be ~~commerated~~ commemorated – shall stand rooted in the ground in names — and

[103]
I say America too must be
    At present what

shall flow in the water in names and be diffused in time, ~~and in~~ in days, in months, in their names. — Now the days signify extinct gods and goddesses — the months ~~long~~ half–unknown rites and emperors — and ~~eh~~ ~~the~~ chronology ~~is~~ with the rest is all foreign to America — All ~~exiles~~ exiles and insults here.

[104]

But it is no small thing, ~~nor easy~~; ~~not a~~ no quick growth; ~~It is~~ not a ~~mere~~ matter of rubbing out one word and ~~of~~ writing another. — ~~The~~ Real names ~~do not~~ never come so easily. — The greatest cities, the greatest politics, the greatest physiology and soul, ~~the~~ ~~p~~ ~~grea~~ the greatest orators, poets, and

literats – The ~~grea~~ best women, the freeest leading men, the proudest national character – such, and the like, are ~~needed~~ indispensable before–hand.
— Then the greatest names will ~~surely~~ follow, // for they are results — and
there are no greater results in the world. —

[105]
Names are the turning point of who shall be master. —
    There is so much virtue in names, that a nation which ~~has~~ produces its
own names, haughtily adheres to them, and subordinates ~~all~~ others ~~th~~ to
them, leads all the ~~others~~ rest of the nations of the earth. — I also promulge
that a nation which has not its own names, but begs them of other nations,
has no identity, ~~is a follower~~ marches not in front but ~~not a leader~~ behind.

[106]
    Names are a test of the esthetic and of spirituality. — ~~The A  The~~ A
delicate ~~and subtle~~ subtle something there is in the right name – an undemonstrable nourishment that ~~soothes a~~ exhilirates ~~and nurishes~~ the soul. ~~with the
undemonstrable nourishment. The masses~~ Masses of men, unaware what
they smoothly [?] ~~like,~~ like, lazily inquire what difference there is between
one name ~~and or~~ and another. — But the few fine ears of the world decide
for them also and recognize them — the masses being always as ~~keen~~ eligible
as any, ~~but even~~ [?] whether they know it or not. —

[107]
    ~~As~~ All that immense volumes, and more than volumes, can tell, are con-
veyed in the right name

The right name of a ~~person~~ city, ~~or~~ state, ~~or~~ town, man, or woman, is a
perpetual feast to the ~~ear.~~ — aesthetic ~~for not th~~ & moral ~~sense~~ nature

[108]
Names of Newspapers:
— What has such a name as The ~~Herald,~~ AEgis, The Mercury or The Herald,
or ~~The Mercury to~~ to do in America?

[109]
    Californian, Texan, New Mexican, and Arizonian names, ~~all~~ have the
sense of the extatic ~~devotee,~~ monk, or ~~nun the breviary,~~ the cloister, the idea
of miracles, and of ~~can men and women~~ devotees canonized after death. —
They are the results of the early missionaries and the element of ~~p~~ piety
in the old Spanish character. — They have, in the same connection, ~~the sense~~

of a ~~curious~~ tinge of melancholy and of a curious freedom from ~~grossness~~
roughness and money–making. ~~They~~ Such names stand strangely in California. — What do ~~such names~~ they know of democracy, of the ~~gold hun~~
[?] hunt for the gold leads, and the nugget or of the religion that is ~~scorn~~
scorn and negation?

[110]

    American writers ~~will~~ are to show far more freedom in the use of words.
— Ten thousand native idiomatic words are growing, or are to–day already
grown, out of which vast numbers could be used by American writers, with
meaning and effect – words that would be ~~dea~~ [?] ~~to~~ welcomed by the
~~people~~ nation, ~~because they are~~ being of the national blood – and would give
that taste ~~and~~ of identity and locality ~~to writing,~~ which is ~~as~~ so dear in
literature. —

## 1

[1]

"Diphthong." — ⟨A literary item.⟩ — The word "diphthong," (to be correctly pronounced ḍif–thong,) is ~~of~~ a word from the Greek, meaning "double ≠ sound." — There are two, Æ and Œ. —

¶The oſd Saxon was full of diphthongs, which we have discarded — thus, for

   brāͤth,   we write   breath
  fāͤ ther    "     "    feather
    dāͤ g                day

~~Th~~   Diphthongs come ⸗ very freely from Greek and Roman words brought into the English language

[2 blank]

[3]

Æ̑ is the Roman or Latin diphthong — also Saxon. — In its affix to old Saxon words it has the sense of the modern term "prestige," or good luck. — Thus Æ dward, (⸗ now Edward) means "prosperous watch," or space of time; Æ dgar, (Edgar,) means successful weapon. — Æ lfred (Alfred) "all peace," &c. —

---

3467. This section of the present volume is made up of 15 different MS notebooks or fragments, all of them in the Feinberg Collection, and though varying in length, they all deal with words or language, or are autobiographical in nature. They are numbered 1 through 15, with the page-numbers I have assigned to them in square brackets. The first one is made up in 10 pages, with writing in Whitman's hand on 5 of them; all of the pages are City of Williamsburgh stationery.

[4 blank]

[5]

Œ is the Greek diphthong. — Its use is generally rejected by modern linguists. — Strictly it belongs as in "œ conomy," and many other words; but we of course write "economy." —
Both these diphthongs are pretty nearly superseded by simple "E." —

[6 blank]

[7]

¶In the latest editions of the great Dictionaries, this ~~supersesion is~~ course is openly announced, as in the following note fromxx Prof. Goodrich's quarto:

[8 blank]

[9]

"Note. — In this work, the diphthongs of foreign words, from which anglicized words are derived, are very often rejected; as in atheneum, maneuver, pean, &c. — The diphthongs ǣ and œ̃ are of difficult formation in writing, and of no use in English words."

[10 blank]

2

[1]      ¶In his presence all the ~~crowns and see~~ Presidents and governors and
         kings of the world bend their heads —

         All wealth and vaunted honor
His eminence ~~makes~~ makes that all sand   however vaunted
         When he appears, Presidents and Governors descend into the crowd,
         ~~for H alone is has eminence; and in its company,~~ capitalists and bank-
         ers are cheap with all their golden eagles. — The learnedest professors,

[2]    /and the ~~makers~~ authors of the ~~best~~ most renowned books ~~are becom~~
       are baffled of their art, ~~and~~ having come to ~~the flowering sweetness~~
       ~~blooming~~ of a great ~~fact~~ fact embodying flower and fruit in nature,
       where ~~they and~~ the ~~best~~ best of ~~them~~ themselves are but the ~~first twit-~~
       ~~tering~~ ? sprouts, groping feebly out of from the February ground. —
       having come to a great fact in the orchard of nature covered with ~~perfec~~
       flowers and fruit, where the best of themselves is but a             feebly
       pushing through the February ground. — /

[3]     The rights of property! Why what build ~~foundation~~ substance is there ~~for the~~ in any other right of property than that which is built on the primal right — the first-born. deepest broadest right — the right of every human being to his personal self. —
     Every man who claims or takes the power to own another man as

[4]  his property, stabs me in ~~that~~ the heart of my own rights — for/they only grow of that first vast principle, as a tree grows from the seed
     Why do we arrest and          a thief of property. — Mainly because in stealing from another man he jeopardizes the principle by why[what?]   you and I and all others hold our own.~~?~~/

[5]     The one scratches me a little on the ~~cheek~~ forehead, the other draws his murderous razor through my heart
     The one mangre [?] all the snivellings of the fash          leaves the man as he found him   solid and real as a       – the other   /

[6]     If every man and woman ~~upon this which~~ riding in this huge huge round car that ~~wheels~~ whirls us through the universe, be not ~~interested in~~ touched to the vitals, by the ~~discussion~~ question whether another of the passengers, ~~can can safely~~ [?] shall be made a slave, tell me O learned lawyer or professor — tell me what are they interested in? — What does touch them? — What comes home to a man, if the principle the right to himself does not? — Is there in the wide world any ~~principle~~ thing, that so evenly and so universally bears upon every indi-

[7]  vidual of our race, in all ages, in/tongues and colors and climates, and conditions. — Is there any thing that it stands us in hand — all of us without exception, ~~are so~~ to keep the rats and ~~wolves~~ moths so carefully away from, as this — the warrantee deed, the original charter of the very feet ~~we stand on?~~ that bear us up

---

     A good saying in the street
     Only something from a gentleman ~~w~~could insult me; and a gentleman never ~~can~~ would insult me.   /

[8]  ☞  ~~Common~~ Good naturally treats every thing — every sect — every dogma — every nation — ~~pen~~ refer to the heart of what goodness there is in them——   /

[9]     [Blank page.]   /

[10]    The difference is between the laws of a just and equitable republic and the laws, even though be the same, that come from an irresponsible tyrant.— /

[11]    I have heard of people who suggest as a choker upon ⌐——— ? ———⌐ the right of freedom that all men are more or less slaves — some to gain, some to fashion, others to priests and superstition. — The hard-working mechanic, they say, is /

[12]    [Blank page.] /

[13]    I know there are strong and solid arguments against slavery — lawyer — practical man — arguments addressed to the great American thought Will it pay? — &c &c &c &c
~~These~~ Discourses ~~upon~~ in this channel entertain and instruct us well

But all these must be now left aside. — We will ascend to ~~that~~ tribunal of last resort — we will not waste words with messengers and

[14]    secretarys. — We will ~~go directly~~ stand face to face with the / chief of the supreme bench. We will speak with the soul. —
The learned think the unlearned an inferior race. — The merchant thinks his bookkeepers and clerks sundry degrees below him; they in turn think the porter and carmen common; and they the laborer that brings in coal, and the stevedores that haul the great burdens with them. /

[15]    But this is an inferior race. — Well who shall be the judge ~~who is the~~ of inferior and superior races. — The class of dainty gentlemen think that all servants and laboring people are inferior. — In all lands, the select few who live and dress richly, ~~always~~ make a mean estimate of the body of the people. —

If it it be ~~right~~ justifiable to take away liberty for inferiority — then

[16]    it is just to take away money or goods, to commit rapes, / to seize on any thing you will, for the same reason. — ~~Would~~ Is it ~~be~~ enough answer to the crime of stealing a watch, that you stole it from an igno-rant nigger, who don't know the odds between an adverb and three times twelve? — If you spend your violent lust on a woman, by terror

and violence, is will it balance accounts receipt the bill when who you endorse it, nothing but a mulatto wench? — /

[17]     But free as great as any worldly wealth to a man, — or her woman-hood to a woman, — greater than these, I think, is the right of liberty, to any and to all men and women. —

It is as logical to take the life or property of some poor fellow for his inferiority or color, as it is to take his personal liberty.— /

[18]     Beware the flukes of the whale. He is slow and sleepy — but when he moves, his lightest touch is death. I think he already feels the lance, for he moves a little restlessly. You are great sportsmen, no doubt What! That black and huge lethargic mass, my sportsmen, dull and sleepy as it seems, has holds the lightning and the belts taps of thunder. — He is slow — O, long and long and slow and slow — but when he does move, his lightest touch is death. /

[19]     The flukes of a whale    they are as quick as light

The Poet
His He has a charm that makes fluid the heart of every thing in the universe however distant or however dense, and when made so he breath inhales it as a breath, and it is all good air arterializes?vitalizes the blood within that goes squirting through his heart.— /[3468]

[20]     The poet, having not a dime, has the good of all things. And men, indeed, only have the good of any thing, in proportion as they enjoy approach the n his nature

The mere rich man, whose draught on the bank for is good for scores of thousands, may be, indeed generally must be, a blind and naked beggar in the the only real riches. of /

[21]     All the riches    ?    evoked  into the world by all the inventors, by the industrious, and by the keen, are become bubbles when the true poet scatters the utterance of his soul upon the world. — To have the crops fail — to forego all the flour and pork of the western states — to burn the navy, or half the a populous town were less to lose, than one of his great sayings to lose. — /

3468.  This entire page has been cancelled by crossed diagonal lines.

[22]    Each word is sweet medicine to the soul. —
He sheds light upon the sun, ~~He~~ on The darkest night he sheds an
infinite darkness.[3469]
You can, to the poet, bring nothing which is not a curious miracle
to him. — /

[23]    Change all this to commendation ☞
What has been called Religion   that of Ethiopia or still backward
— that of Belus and Osiris and Isis, or that of — or that of Jerusalem
with its temple an           — that of Rome under Popes and Jesuits
— that of Mahomet or Bhudda — ~~Par~~ those of our Methodists and
Epi[s]copalians and Presbyterians and Quakers and Unitarians and
Mormons — what are they ~~any or~~ all or any of them? ~~We~~ I know they
are intrinsically little or nothing, though nations and ages have writhed
for ~~most of~~ them in life and in death. — ~~We~~ I know they do not satisfy.

[24]    the appetite of  /  the soul, with all their churches and their libraries
and their priesthood. — Nevertheless let us treat them with decent for-
bearance. Mean as they are when we have ascended beyond them, and
look back, they were doubtless the roads for their times, — ~~and~~   Let
us not ~~despise~~ too quickly despise them; — for they have ~~brought~~
sufficed to bring us where we are. —
Like scaffolding which is a blur and nuisance when the house is well
up — yet the house could not be achieved without the scaffold. —   /

3

[1]    No doubt the efflux of the soul ~~is~~ comes through beautiful gates of
laws that ~~we may~~ at some future period perhaps a few score millions
of years, we may understand better. — At present, its tide is what ~~we~~
folks call capricious, and cannot well be traced.*(   ) — Why as I just
~~catch a~~ look in the railroad car at some ~~workman's~~ half turned face, do
I love that ~~being~~ woman? Though~~xxx~~ But she is neither young nor
~~beautiful~~ fair ~~featured~~ complexioned? — /She remains in my memory
afterward for a year, and I calm myself to sleep at night by thinking of
her. — Why ~~are~~ be there men I meet, and ~~many~~ others I know, that

[2]    ~~when~~ while they are with me, the sunlight of Paradise / ~~warms~~

3469.  This passage has been cancelled by crossed diagonal lines.

expands my blood — that ~~if~~ when I walk with an arm of theirs around
my neck, my soul ~~leaps and laughs like a new-waked child~~ scoots and
courses like ~~a caressed~~ an unleashed dog ~~caressed~~ — that when they
leave me the pennants of my joy sink flat ~~from the~~ and lank in the
deadest calm? —

Why ~~do I as I sit at my table in~~ do flocks of ~~thoughts,~~ ideas, some
twittering as wrens or chirping or ~~robins~~ peeshouts,? some soft as
pigeons, some screaming as ~~eagles~~ sea-hawks, some shy and afar off as
the wild brant, some invariably why do these ~~swarms~~ beat their count-

[3]   less wings and clutch / their feet upon me, as I sit ~~in the adjoining
room,~~ near by ~~to~~ where my brother is practising at the piano? [3470] —
There is a certain block between my house and the South ferry, not
especially different from other blocks ~~densely~~[?] bordered by trees:
Why ~~then~~ do I never pass ~~it~~ there without new and large and ~~beautiful~~
melodious ~~thoughts~~ thoughts descending upon me? — ~~I think~~ I guess
they may there winter and summer pry[?] the limbs off those trees and
continually drop the point[?] ~~upon~~ if I travel that ~~blaze~~[?] way. Some
fisherman that ~~always stop to pass the time o day with,~~ give good morning to and pass ten or twenty minutes as he draws his seine by the shore
— some carpenter working his ripsaw through a plank — some driver,
as I ride on top of the stage, — men rough, ~~rough,~~ not handsome, not
accomplished — why do I know that the subtle chloro-/form of our

[4]   spirits is affecting each other, and though we may ~~never meet~~ encounter
not again, ~~we know feel that we two~~ have ~~pass~~ exchanged the right
~~mysterious unspoken~~ password ~~of the night,~~ and ~~have~~ are thence free
~~entrance~~ comers to ~~each~~ the guarded tents of each others' ~~love~~ most
interior love?

*(What is the ~~cause~~ meaning, any how, of my ~~love attachment~~
adhesiveness ~~for~~ toward others? — What is the cause of their ~~love for~~
toward ~~for~~ me?) — (Am I loved by them boundlessly because my love
for them is more boundless? —) /

[5]       While the curtain is down at the opera, while I swim in the bath,
while I wait for my friend at the corner, while I ~~visit swim in the bath,~~
I behold and am beheld by people ~~men and women;~~ I speak little or
nothing; I ~~offer~~ make no gifts to them: I do not turn as much as my

3470.  Whitman bought a piano for his brother Jeff on 10 January 1852 (receipt in the
Feinberg Collection).

neck or pat my ~~boot~~ instep ~~in their behalf~~ to gain m[?] t[?] ~~from them~~;
of the fatter[?]; we never met ~~nor~~ before — never heard ~~of~~ or shall
hear ~~each's each's other before~~ names nor dates nor employments. —
With all this, some god walks in noiseless and resistless, ~~takes~~ and takes
their hearts out of their breasts, and gives them to me for ever. — Often
I ~~see it, and get~~ catch the ~~hint~~, sign; and oftener, no doubt, it ~~goes over
me~~ flies by me as unknown as my neighbor's dreams. — [3471]  /

[6]   and bring her naked to his bed, that ~~he~~ they ~~together~~ may sleep together
~~with her~~; and she shall come again whenever he will, and the taste shall
~~always~~ be sweeter and sweeter always)   President ~~L- Their~~ Their
Rules and their Pets!   I see them lead him ~~onward~~ now. — I see ~~the~~
his large slow gait, his face illuminated ~~and gay~~ like the face of a ~~happy~~
young child. — ~~I see him shooting the light of his soul~~ Onward he
moves with the gay procession ~~to the and the band music of of laughter~~
laughing pioneers and the wild trilling bugles of joy. — Onward he
moves with the gay procession, and the laughing pioneers, and the
wild-trilling bugles of joy  /

[7]   <u>The Poet</u>
I think His sight is the sight of the     ? (bird  and his scent the
instinct of the     ? dog   I think ten million supple-fingered gods
are perpetually employed hiding beauty in the world — ~~hiding~~ burying
it everywhere in everything — ~~but~~ and most of all ~~where~~ in spots that
men and women do not think of ~~it~~, and never look — as ~~in~~ death. —
Cache ~~after~~ and cache ~~again they is~~ all over the earth, and in the heavens ~~above~~    that swathe the earth, and in the ~~dep~~ waters of the sea. —
~~Their~~ They do their ~~task~~ jobs well; those ~~supple fingered gods.~~ journey-

[8]   men divine. ~~But~~ Only ~~to~~ from the poet ~~do can~~ they can hide nothing;
~~hide.~~ — and would not if they could. — Him they ~~attend~~ wait on night
and day and ~~show where they take~~ uncover all, that he shall see the
naked breast and the most private        ~~of Delight.~~ —
I ~~think~~ reckon he is ~~the really the god~~ Boss of those gods; ~~for they~~
and the work they do is done for him, and all that they have concealed
for his ~~sake~~ sake — ~~Ahead For~~ Him they attend outdoors or indoors;
~~to his perceptions they open all.~~ — They ~~ru~~ run ~~sensibly~~[?] ahead ~~as~~
when he walks, ~~and to~~ and lift their cunning covers, and ~~poi~~ signify
~~to~~ him with ~~points~~ pointed stretched arms. — ~~The The~~ (They undress
Delight  /

3471.  This page and the next seven are each cancelled by crossed diagonal lines.

[9]    What variety what richness in life:
But ~~grea~~ richer than life ~~is~~ spreads out what we call Day[?]
How supple is youth,
How muscular, how full of love and grace and unspeakable fascination,
But old age may wear ~~more love and~~ graces and fascinations a thousand
    fold.
How large and splendid is the sunlit day
Till the night comes with ~~its mystery and darkness~~ transparent dark-
    ness and mystery and the stars,
~~And those t~~Touching the soul closer than the grandest day
How magnificent ~~are riches~~ is wealth ~~that spread over one~~ affording

[10]    gifts ~~with out stint~~ from the  /  ample hand, and superb clothes
    and hospitality
But all ~~riches are~~ wealth is nothing to the soul's, which ~~are~~ is candor
    ~~and life~~ and ~~all~~ enfolding love,
Did not Jesus show that what we call poverty is ~~great~~ the greatest ~~riches~~
    wealth?  /

[11]    Why what is this curious little ~~thing creature~~ thing ~~you~~ you ~~pr~~ hold
~~out~~ before us? — ~~We read in the advertisements of your new and
edition our the race enlarge and improved.~~ Do you call ~~this such an
this~~ such an ~~abject~~ wretched ~~thing~~ creature as you have pictured here a
man? — ~~A~~ Man is the resident of the earth. ~~Why~~ This is no man of
the ~~whole~~ earth. — This is ~~some~~ the abject louse — ~~some~~ the milk-faced

[12]    maggot  /    What an abject creature    ~~would~~ make a ~~human
being~~ man. — Notice! What louse is this ~~you~~ what ~~crawling~~ milk faced
~~snivelling~~ maggot, that ~~falls lays~~ flattens itself upon the ground,
and asks leave to live, ~~as of no~~ not as of right of its own, but by special
favor; ~~snufflin~~ snivelling how it ~~is~~ were righteously condemned, being
of the vermin race, and ~~is~~ will ~~crawl~~ be only too thankful ~~to go to its~~
if it ~~be let~~ can ~~crawl escape creep hole under the dung, and escape~~
dodge the stick or booted heel, and escape to its hole under the dung!   /

[13]    I should think poorly of myself if I ~~could~~ should be even a few days
with any community either of sane or insane people, and not make
them convinced, whether they acknowledged it or not, ~~with~~ of my
truth, my sympathy, and my dignity. — I should be ~~assured~~ certain
enough that those attributes were not in me. — ~~The~~ Although it may
balk and tremble a few moments on its   balance? it ~~is~~ will surely
signify  /

[14]      No piety that macerates and flogs itself, and refuses women and laughter and a ~~rich florid~~ long strong florid life, ~~is equal~~ begins to be piety in comparison with that which
          If your souls do not
The most accomplished lapidary cannot ~~tell~~ separate the real opal an ? and from their counterfeits in glass, ~~as~~ so unerringly as the soul can tell what is its truth and what is sham. — Yet in the ~~superb~~ ordinations, this clarifying and separating power, in any thing like perfection is not arrived at ~~in anything like perfection,~~ hastily. — Nature is not a young fellow*  /

[15]      In the city when the streets have been long neglected, they heap up banks of mud in the shape of graves, and put boards at the head and feet, with very significant inscriptions. —
          Comparison between a sincere devotee of any time, and a fashionable preacher. —
          O yes the Fugitive Slave Law is obeyed northerly every day in the year — except three hundred and sixty five  /

[16]      All this Religion of the world  –    –    as it is let us not be too stern with it — it is the meagre grass thin and pale and yellow which shows the life of the soil; ~~and~~
          A bell ringer went out at night to sound his alarm for a fire. — After two or three rings, the notes ceased, and when they went to see, the bell ringer was dead. —  /

[17]  ~~are be~~ become[?] ready. —
          amplitude of her means, x time is inconceivably ample. — ~~Therefore~~ It is for She does not rush, ~~and~~ not get in any tight spot that needs hard scratching
          Give me the commander who carries a thousand regiments in his breast — both horses[?] foot; in his head — and whole packs of artillery, the swiftest and best disciplined in the world  /

[18]      Comes some one to a man saying, your mother is famished, your brother is blue and dead with cold, and the man answers, I have ~~xx~~ meat, but it is inconvenient to go for it just now; and I have cloth, but it is out of reach on a ~~high~~ shelf  / [3472]

3472. The top half of these two pages has been clipped out of the notebook; the bottom paragraph on the first page has been cancelled by diagonal crossed lines.

[19]     Inescapably curious is ~~the con~~ what we call happiness. — I have felt the ~~strange~~ sweet mystery more for forty minutes cleaning and gresing[?] my boots, than

Has what I have said [?] an          seized upon you soul and set its sign there          If not then I know there is no elementary vigor in my ~~the~~ words If ~~it have~~ not, then I throw my words ~~with~~ among the other parings and crusts of the swill tub, and go home and bathe myself, and listen to music, and touch my lips to the flesh of sleeping children, an come and try again. /

[20]     The Poet

What you call your Religion, ~~however warm it may~~ – paint ~~it as~~ with as much red as you can stick on — wrench the biggest words ~~to~~ to describe it — and then multiply many fold; ~~yet~~ it is yet too ~~feeble~~ feeble and ~~cold~~ babyish for the Poet. — He ~~must~~ will have something infinitely more alive and ample and strong and fiery and comprehensive. —

There is an ugliness undone and unspoken, worse than ~~the~~ any sins of ignorance or ~~bad temper~~ uncouth ways. — A man shall maliciously tell of ~~some~~ the chap at the table picking his teeth with the dinner fork, and show

[21]     ~~This hat~~ thus bring a little hood and ~~coat~~ tunic ~~you have~~ tailored ~~too small~~ for ~~the soul is~~ for some ~~wilted~~[?] ~~sickly~~ poor consumptive ~~wasted~~[?] child, and you bring your clothier's tapes gaudy with spangles of tin. — [3473]

For thy soul, ~~that is so~~ and whose far spreading ~~breasts~~ shoulders burst ~~large that~~ the overcoat of the universe, as ~~inconceivably too~~ insupportably ~~cramping~~ pinching and scant, and of ~~no~~ small account — ~~that~~ who ~~t~~ takes the suns for its ~~toys~~ toys, and soon wants ~~something~~ better — ~~they will~~ you ~~bring piece~~ tailor up the little hood and tunic ~~tailored for~~ sizable to some poor consumptive child, and ~~made~~ horribly gaudy with spangles of tin?

---

an ill bred ~~soul~~ heart far ~~worse than~~ more dismal than any want of etiquette. / [3474]

[22]     ¢Looking to the ~~outer~~ scrofulous politics ~~whose~~ of Europe, and what

3473. This paragraph has been cancelled by two diagonal lines.
3474. This line is actually the last part of the sentence on the previous page, which ends there, ". . . the dinner fork, and show".

comes thence, ~~Men~~ folks think it ~~a~~ dismal ~~thing when the kings~~ that some king or kings daughter, ~~un~~ unseated from their thrones and exiled, should pine and linger, and be starved of the grand ~~presus-tenance~~ which honors and prerogatives of

But all

---

Greatness is simply development.  /

[23]    ~~Shall Does~~ The clothier comes supercilious ~~and swallow-tailed~~ swallow-tailed, ~~wh with~~ and flirts his measuring, tape, ~~and shears~~ for ~~the~~ my Soul ~~whose~~ — my Soul ~~that,~~ with far-~~stretching~~ bulging shoulders bursting the overcoat of the ~~universe~~ heavens as insupportably pinching and scant — ~~who takes fiery suns for toys, and soon wants something brighter;~~ — and ~~can~~ will the ~~swallow-tailed gentleman~~ loud promising gentleman duly send home to me nothing better than this little tunic for some poor consumptive child — this baby hood, with spangles of tin?  /

[24]    I think ten million supple-~~fingered~~ wristed gods are ~~perpetually~~ always ~~employed~~ hiding beauty in the world — burying it every where in every thing — and most of all in spots that men and women do not think of and never look — as Death and Poverty and Wickedness. — Cache! and Cache again!  all over the earth, and in the heavens that swathe the earth, and in the waters of the sea. — They do their jobs well; those journeymen divine. Only from the Poet they can hide nothing and would not if they could. — I reckon he is Boss of those gods; and the work they do is done for him; and all they have concealed, they have concealed for his sake. — Him they attend indoors and outdoors. — They run ahead when he walks, and lift their cunning covers and signify him with pointed stretched arms.

Their President and their Pet! I see them lead him now. — I see his large, slow gait — his face illuminated like the face of an arm-bound child. Onward he moves with the gay procession, and the laughing pioneers, and the wild trilling bugles of joy.— / [3475]

4

[1]                              "wood drake" [3476]
     "Summer Duck or "Wood Duck", very gay, including in its colors

---

3475.  This page has been cancelled by crossed diagonal lines.
3476.  The following notes on birds, nature, Greek dramatists, and other matters were

white, red, yellow, green, blue, &c crowns violet — length 20 inches
— common in the United States — often by ~~creeks~~ streams and
ponds — rises and slowly circuits — selects hollow trees to breed in
— keeps in parties — generally move in pairs at least

King Bird "Tyrant Flycatcher" length 8½ inches — loud shrill voice
— attacks hawks and crows as if for amusement — when tired it
retreats to some stake or limit, with a triumphant twitter. —

Peewee — one of the earliest comers in spring — builds nest often
under the eaves of a deserted house or barn — pleasing note —

"Redstart" — beautiful small bird arrives here latter part of April,
returns south late in September — common in woods and along
roadside and meadow — feeds on insects — active — has a lively
twitter. —

☞  All the above are met on Long Island.

Young squaw
Papoose — old squaw

One personal deed, on one ~~great~~ effusion of some grand strength
and will of man — may go far beyond law, custom, and all other con-
ventionalism — and seize upon the heart of the whole race, utterly
defiant of authority or argument against ~~them~~ it. —

Do you suppose the world is finished, at any certain time — like a
contract for paving a street? — Do you suppose because the American
government has been formed, and public schools established, we have
nothing more to do but take our ease, and make money, and ~~let things
grow~~ sleep out the rest of the time?

Fear ~~delectation delicatesse~~ grace!    Fear ~~grace!~~ delicatesse! — ~~dl~~
del-i-ca-tésse — These precede the (what is it in fruit when just ripe)
terrible ripeness of nature — the decay of the ruggedness of ~~a~~ men —
~~the~~ and of ~~a~~ nations. —    /

[2]  Go on! go on! we ha'n't got time

Ens — 1 a being, existence essence, that recondite part of a substance
from which all its qualities flow (old term in metaphysics*

written by Whitman on both sides of two lined sheets torn from a tall notebook (one of
the sheets torn in half). The opening words may have been used in "Song of Myself," Section 13, lines 237–243, which read:
My tread scares the wood-drake and wood-duck of my distant and day-long ramble,
They rise together, they slowly circle around.

I believe in those wing'd purposes,
And acknowledge red, yellow, white, playing within me,
And consider green and violet and the tufted crown intentional.
(*Leaves of Grass,* Comprehensive Reader's Edition, p. 40)

———— Look out there's

"Take heed to yourselves — there's a mad man ~~stalking~~ loose through in the ship, with a knife in his hands," — such was the warning sung out at night more than once below in the Old Jersey prison ship, 1780 moored at the Wallabout in the Revolution. — Utter derangement was a frequent symptom of the aggravated sickness that prevailed there. — The prisoners were allowed no light at night. — No physicians were ~~allowed~~ provided. —

Sophocles, Eschylus, and Euripides flourished about the time of the birth of Socrates 468 B. C. and years afterwards. — Great  as their remains are, they were transcended by other works that have not come down to us. — Those other works, often gained the first prizes. —

In Eschylus the figures are shadowy, vast, and majestic dreaming, moving with haughty grandeur, strength and will

In Sophocles, the dialogue and feelings are more like reality and the interest approaches home — great poetical beauty. —

In Euripides, love and compassion — scientific refinement, — something like skepticism. — This writer was a hearer of Socrates. —

Phallic festivals — Wild mirthful processions in honor of the god Dionysus (Bacchus), in Athens, and other parts of Greece — unbounded license — mocking jibes and irony — epithets and biting insults

To the Poor —

I have my place among you

Is it nothing that I have preferred to be poor rather than to be rich?

The road to riches is easily open to me,

But I do not choose it.

I choose to stay with you. —   /

[3]    (bring in a few. . . .of ancient and modern times — the words I can find and the most cruel and their ~~oper effects~~ practical operations.)

Does any one tell me that it is the part of a man to obey such enactments as these?

I tell you the world is demented with this very obedience —

When a man, untrammeling himself from blind obedience to ~~pries~~ the craft of priests and politicians, branches out with his own sovereign will and strength — knowing that ~~himself~~ the unspeakable greatness of himself, or of the meanest of his fellow creatures — expands far beyond all the laws and governments of the earth — then he begins really to be a man. — Then he is great. —

From the baldness of birth to the baldness of burials and shrouds

Something behind or afterward. — Leave the impression that no matter what is said, there is something greater to say — something behind still more marvelous and beautiful —     / ³⁴⁷⁷

[4]          He does better with spare. . . .out hunger, great starvation, op-posing enemies, contentions

Riches — It is only the mean and vulgar appetite that craves money and property as the first and foremost of its wants

I have appeared among you to say that all what [    ]do     is right, and that what you affirm is right;

                                             ?

But that it is they are only the alphabet of right. —
And that you shall use them as beginnings and first attempts. —
I have not appeared to take any with violent hands to pull up by the roots any thing that has grown,
Whatever has grown, has grown well. —
Do you suppose fancy there was is any some flaw water in the semen of the first perpetual copulation?
Do you of believe suppose the celestial laws of universe might be re-formed and rectified?     / ³⁴⁷⁸

5 ³⁴⁷⁹

                gr
[1]     med Cophōsis, deafness, dumbness, or dullness of any sense
                gr
       med Cōpos, a morbid lassitude
           Sensorium, the seat of sensation, doubtless the brain
           Liaison (lé-a-zohn), a binding or fastening together
           Because women do not appear in history or philosophy with any-thing like the same prominence as men — that is no reason for treating them less than men: — The great names that we know are but the acci-dental scraps. — Mention to me the twenty grea most majestic charac-ters that have existed upon the earth, and have their names recorded. — It is very well. — But for that twenty, there are millions upon mil-

---

3477.  The top half of this page and the next one is missing.
3478.  The bottom of this sheet is torn, with three words showing: ". . . and about Vice?"
3479.  The material in this selection was written by Whitman on both sides of two lined sheets torn from a tall notebook.

lions just as great, whose names are unrecorded. — It was in them to do ~~grander~~ actions as grand — to say as beautiful thoughts — to set ~~the~~ examples for their race. — But in each one the book was not opened. — It lay in its place ready

The greatest and truest knowledge can never be taught or passed over from him or her who has it, to him or her who has it not. — It is in the soul. — It is not susceptible of proof or ~~demon~~ explanation. — It applies to all things and encloses them. — ~~All that there The enti is in what~~ What men think enviable, if it ~~were~~ could be collected together for ten thousand years, would not be of the least account, compared with this wisdom. — It is the ~~sight of the~~ consciousness of the reality and excellence of every thing. — It is happiness. — ~~Every~~ Each and ~~every~~ each woman is eligible to it, without education just ~~the~~ as readily as with whoever reads these words, let him or her set out upon the search this day,. ~~and never rest till~~

My Lesson[3480]

Have you learned ~~the~~ my lesson complete:
It is well — it is but the gate to a larger lesson — and
~~And~~ that to another: ~~still~~
And ~~every one of us~~ each successive one to another still
Poem "Praise of things" [3481]  /

[2]  *(down)   spor-a-des, scattered islands, stars, &c
Play?

Novel? — Work of some sort_∧ — instead of sporadic characters — introduce them in large masses, on a far grander scale — armies — twenty-three full-formed perfect athletes — orbs — take characters through the orbs — "spiritualism" Nobody appears upon the stage simply — but all in huge aggregates   nobody speaks alone — whatever is said, is said by an immense number

<u>Shade</u> — And twenty-five old men  old man with rapid gestures — eyes black and flashing like lightning — long white beard — attended by an immense train — <u>no</u> warriors or warlike weapons or helmets — all emblematic of peace — shadowy — rapidly ~~approaches and pauses~~ sweeping by — if in a play — let the descriptions ~~not~~ that

3480.  Notes for "Who Learns My Lesson Complete?": see *Leaves of Grass,* Comprehensive Reader's Edition, pp. 393–395.
3481.  Compare "His thoughts are the hymns of the praise of things," "By Blue Ontario's Shore," Section 10, line 14, *Leaves of Grass,* Comprehensive Reader's Edition, p. 348.

are usually put in brief, in brackets, in italics, be also in poetry, carefully finished as the dialogue

<u>The answerer</u>[3182]

<u>Plot for a Poem or other work</u> — A manly unpretensive philosopher — without any of the old insignia, such as age, books ~~eth~~ etc. — a fine-formed person, of beautiful countenance, &c. — Sits every day at the door of his house —To him for advice come all sorts of people. — Some come to puzzle him — some come from curiosity — some from ironical contempt — his answers — his opinions

¶ 2  A man appears in public every day — Every time he appears with a companion — one day it is a beautiful youth — another time with a voluptuous woman — another time with a poor pale emaciated sick person, whom he has brought out for a little air — another

☞  good subject ⎫ — Variety of characters, each one of whom comes
      Poem ⎬ forth every day — things appearing, transfers and
           ⎭ promotions every day.

There was a child went forth every day — and the first things that he ~~saw~~ looked at with fixed love, that thing he became for the day. —[3483]

* Bring in whole races, or castes, or generations, to express themselves — personify the general objects of the creative and give them voice — every thing on the most august scale — a leaf of grass, with its equal voice. —

☞ — voice of the generations of slaves — of those who have suffered — voice of Lovers — of Night — Day — Space — the stars — the countless ages of the Past — the countless ages of the future  /


[3]                    (A <u>spiritual novel</u>?
<u>Man's Muscular capability</u>. Phren. Jour. vol 7, page 96

( <u>A tradition</u> —)that to eat the meat of serpents is restorative and helps longevity  In writing, the same taste and law as in personal demeanor — that is never to strain, or exhibit the least apparent desire to make <u>stick out</u> the pride, grandeur, and boundless richness — but to <u>be</u> those,

3482.  Compare "Song of the Answerer," *Leaves of Grass,* Comprehensive Reader's Edition, pp. 166–170.
3483.  Compare "There Was a Child Went Forth," *Leaves of Grass,* Comprehensive Reader's Edition, pp. 364–366, especially lines 1–4:
There was a child went forth every day,
And the first object he look'd upon, that object he became,
And that object became part of him for the day or a certain part of the day,
Or for many years or stretching cycles of years.

and let the spirit of them vitalize whatever is said

In writing, give no second hand articles — no quotations — no authorities — <u>give the real</u> thing — ready money —

A poem in which all things and qualities and processes express themselves — the nebula — the fixed stars — the earth — the grass, waters, vegetable, sauroid, and all processes — man — animals.[3484]

Can a man be wise without he get wisdom from the books?

Can he be religious and have nothing to do with churches or prayers?

Can he have great style, without being dressed in fine clothes and without any name or fame?

In writing, every thing is to be brought in in its <u>human</u> relations — this invariably. — It is not needful that this should be made palpable to all ages — but it must <u>be,</u> and it must act supreme in all the plot or course of writing. —

---

A large stone cavity, exactly cut out — in this is placed a man — he has plenty to eat — he has whatever he asks for — money unbounded is around him — but there he lives — he walks around carrying with him that portable impenetrable stone coffin. —

---

"String team" — the horses, — three, four, or five — in single file, without curb or bit, that draw the cars, or other vehicles — the peculiar manner of calling to 'em and directing them — "Black Jack's" illustrations of the way of guiding them —    /

[4]    You are one of

The common statesman thinks of men as people to be governed — thinks a government a great thing in itself — takes much care about checks and balances — offices — &c. —

You are

The common philosopher maps out his system, fortifies it by powerful argument — proves how it is true — how much better than all ~~that~~ the rest of its rivals — &c.

Do not fancy — that I have come to descend among you, gentlemen. — I encompass you all

<u>A rule or two invariable in personal and literary demeanor.</u> — <u>Never</u> to complain of any attacks or harsh criticism upon myself, or my writings — never to defend either by a single word or argument —

---

3484.  This paragraph is set off by horizontal lines.

never to deprecate any one's enmity or opposition — nor vindicate my-self. — Not to suppose or recognize ~~the~~ as a possible occurrence, that it can be necessary for me to <u>prove</u> I am right ~~and great~~ or clean. —

It is only the common ambition that is satisfied with the eminence that comes from wealth or office. — Far above these is the eminence of personal qualities — a grand prescence — wit — conversational power — that charm, we don't know what it is, which goes with the mere face and body magnetism of some men and women and makes every body love them, wherever they go. — Even the movements of one's limbs, and the gestures of the hands are ~~great~~ can fascinate. — ~~But all~~ That which comes from the mere possession of riches, is ~~little. — It is~~ rather a blur upon the highest ~~action; it is~~ forms of humanity

### A Crayon in brief

An illu~~stration.~~ — ∧ Socrates, sauntering through the market place, attracted by the princely youth of Athens — cross-questioning — his big paunch — his bare feet — his subtle tongue —   /

## 6

## An Early Notebook

[Inside front cover]

16th Sept

G. L. Metcalf
    3^d district Station house
      ~~3^d ward~~   79 Warren

Organism of Language
      Becker's
    Translated into English

Grimm's Work on German Language

W. Gibson
    363 Sixth av

Middlesex House
      Concord, Mass

Dr. Ruggles
    24 East Warren

Wilson
    4 Greene
            near Cumberland
       Pond [ ? ]

[Flyleaf]

    A. Bronson Alcott
        Oct. 4th '56

Jas Metcalf
    79 Warren st. (station house)

Mr. Held
    4 Boerum
        near Fulton av.

Clerke's Rudiments
       & Practice
   1 vol

    comic Blackstone

Prof Wines'
  Commentary on the
        Hebrew Law

Montesquieu
    Spirit of the Laws

Robert Hunt's
    "Poetry of Science"

Poetry of the East
    Pub Wittemore, Niles & Hall
                  Boston

[Inside flyleaf]

"Ancient Hebrews"
        by Abm. Mills
   A. S. Barnes & Co.

"Glimpses of Life & Manners
        in Persia"
    by Lady Sheil
with notes on Russia, Koords,
    Turkomans, Nestorians,
            (refers to 1849)

_____

    Mrs Tyndale
            at Mrs. Manning's
~~at~~ in Clinton av.
            near De Kalb
Nearly opposite the church

_____

Dr. Draper's Physiology
        (Harper
        last 2 no(s
                Harper)

_____

Brownlow's Map of the Stars
            184 Cherry st.

[1]

⟍ Sam Matthews ⟋
    Walt Whitman stands to–day
in the midst of the American people,
a promise, a preface, an
overture a
    Will he fulfill the half–distinct
half–indistinct promise? —
Many do not understand him,
but there are others, a few, who
do understand him~~?~~    Will
he justify the great prophecy
of Emerson?    Or will he
too, like thousands of others,
            one
flaunt out ~~the~~    bright
commencement, the result of
gathered powers, only to sink
back exhausted – or to
give himself up to the seduction
of

[2 blank]

[3 cut in half]
    The observer stand ~~some~~
clear day on the northeast
height of Washington Park,
some clear day in the year
1900, (the year of These
States,) will look on

[4 cut in half, blank]

[5 cut in half]
? For your own sake
To stand fast by me!
To stand unshaken, ~~and~~
        tenacious, — ~~to~~

~~To believe in me — no-
        matter~~

[6 cut in half, blank]

[7]
    I had rather have the
good will of the butchers and
boatman of Manhattan Island
than all the nominations
            approbation
            rewards
of the government – literats
    elegant  persons
    ~~fake~~

[8 blank]

[9–12 clipped out]

[13–16 cut in half, blank]

[17]
    American songs,

— in which prose,
(to be spoken – with a
low, or other musical
accompaniament,) is interlineated

[18  blank]

[19 top third clipped out]
Primer of words
    ~~and Th~~ and
      Thoughts ⎫ None of
      Ideas    ⎬  these
      Principles ⎭   suit

[20 top third clipped out, blank]

[21 top three-quarters clipped out]

———————————

Have you any doubt of mortality?
I say there can be no more
    doubt of immortality than
    there is of mortality

[22 top three-quarters clipped out, blank]

[23 top half clipped out]
For friendship
        :

–    –    –    –

For immortality :

[24 top half clipped out, blank]

[25]
Poem of Maternity

———————

O my dear child!   My
    Darling
(Now I am maternal –
    a child bearer –

~~I bea~~ have from
my womb borne
a child, and
observe it

~~For great ideas!~~
The life that is not
    underlaid by great
    ideas is - —

[26 blank]

[27]
        In  Poem
            model of poems
The earth,    ~~that is my~~
            ? none need
    ~~model - I do not~~
    discard what I
    find in the theory
            diversified
    of the great, round
    earth, so beautiful, ~~and~~
        so rude.
The body of a man, ⌿ that
    ⌿ is my model - I do
    not reject what I
    find in my body - I
    am not ashamed - Why
    should I be ashamed?
The body of a woman, ⌿
    that is my perfect
    model - I believe
    in all the body of
    the woman - I believe
    the perfect woman
    shall even precede
    the man

[28 blank]

[29]
Personality!
You! whoever you are!
    without one single

    exception, in any
    part of any of These
    States!
   ?
I ~~seize~~ you with ~~st~~
    free and severe ~~your~~
    hand – I know well,
whoever you are,
    you are my equal,
    and the President's
    equal, – and that there
    is no one on this
    globe ~~and~~ any ~~better~~
    ~~gr~~ greater than you –
    and that there is
    no existence in all
    the universes any more
    immortal than youxx,


[30 blank]

[31]
~~Free~~
Personality!
Your Personality! You
    ~~and~~ whoever you are?
O you coward that
    dare not ~~classic~~
    be audacious ~~for~~
    ~~your own sake!~~
O you liar that
    ~~falsely~~ assume to
    be modest and
    deferential
O you slave
    tongueless,

O you eyeless, earless,
-O you          that
          will not receive me
          for your own sake

[32 blank]

[33]
Great ideas dominate
____ over all –
What has Shakespeare
____ done to England?
Not    –    –    not    –    –
          are of any account
          compared to the
          few men of great
____ ideas
Even
     One great idea vitalizes
____ a nation
— Men of great ideas

[34]
This then ∤ is life, and
          this is the earth. –
How curious! How real.
Underfoot, the divine soil, —
          o
Ө verhead, the sun[3485]
     ?       my
Surround ~~these~~ poems, you
          east and west, for
          they are for you

____

3485. Compare "Starting from Paumanok," Section 2, lines 4–7, *Leaves of Grass,* Comprehensive Reader's Edition, p. 16:
     This then is life,
     Here is what has come to the surface after so many throes and convulsions,

     How curious! how real!
     Underfoot the divine soul, overhead the sun.

And you north and
      south, for they are
      for you,[3486]
Imbue them, nights, for
      they are (of you, and
      for you,
And you, days, for they
      are for you. —
Lo


[35 top two-thirds clipped out]
Do you not know that
      your
      ~~the~~ soul has brothers
      and sisters, just as
         your
      much as the body
      has?


[36 top two-thirds clipped out]
    ~~my~~ (ancestors, of man
      you
Nor ~~you, you~~   ~~the~~
      old poets
I do not forget to salute
      you
  you, ~~you, old~~ poets,
     ages
  of all ~~times~~ and
  lands,


[37 top third clipped out]

How real is the ground!


3486. Compare "Starting from Paumanok," Section 4, lines 1–4, *Leaves of Grass,* Comprehensive Reader's Edition, p. 17:
    Take my leaves America, take them South and take them North,
    Make welcome for them everywhere for they are your own off-spring,
    Surround them East and West, for they would surround you,
    And you precedents, connect lovingly with them, for they connect lovingly with you.

Come let us ~~p~~ set
our feet upon the
ground;
How perfect and beautiful
are the animals!
~~How vas~~
How much room, and
splendor!    How inevitable
How ~~vast and~~ spacious!

[38 top third clipped out]
~~shall ought to~~ deserves
~~to~~ ∧ ~~receive~~ more than
you, and never can
deserve

fail
I do not ~~forget~~ to
with my hand
salute you, you            and neck
poets of all ages
and lands,
I do not forget ~~to bless~~
any one of
you,      you fallen
to bless you –
nations, — nor any
one of you, ~~you~~
ancestors of men

[39 top half clipped out]
How curious is the brown
~~wa~~ real earth!
How curious, how
spiritual is the water

Politics
On the one side pledged
to      —    —    —
On the other side to

—    —    —

– On the one side – – – –
on

[40 top half clipped out]
I understand you, you
     bards of other ~~ages, and~~ lands
   bear you in mind,
I ~~understand you~~, you
    ancestors of men. —

[41 bottom half clipped out]
Lo!   ~~the~~ ships sailing!
           intersecting
Lo, ~~the the interminable~~
   streets in cities, full
   of living people, coming
   and going!
Lo, ~~where~~ iron and steam,
    so grand, so welcome!
Lo, ~~w~~

[42 bottom half clipped out, blank]

[43–46 clipped out]

[Notebook was turned over and started again from the back; pagination thus starts anew.]

[Inside back cover]

    9th av. cor 24th
     Dan Van Valkenb

Lot on Lawton st near
      Division av
  W. McCormick
     105 Byard st
S. Walling
     LeRoy Place
       Bleeker St

Silas Ludlan

   Youngmans
    63 2[d] av.

F. Bellew
    70 West 27<sup>th</sup> St

Empire House –
    Pennsylvania av between
        3<sup>d</sup> & 4th street

Mrs. Harrison's
        Pennsylvania

[Flyleaf]

            [?]
Patrick Fleming, Jackson Hall Alley
        & Pennsylvania
Dr. Smith,           av
    xxxxxxxxxxxxxxxxxxxx
    Charles Drummond
140 York st. cor. Charles

    Mrs. Tyndale
    Germantown
      cor Main and
        High sts. —

Mrs. Chilton    Phebe Ann
              Wood
    69 Varick st.  348  Grove

Mr. T. C. Leland,
    77 Duane st.

Mrs. Walton
    107, Dean, corner
        Hoyt.

John W. Usher
Cor Pensylvania av & 14  th st
    City Lunch

[Inside flyleaf blank]

[1–2 clipped out]

[3 bottom two-thirds clipped out]
    N. Y. Express, Oct. 21, 1856
  "But for the American party,
the Northern, sectional, geographical
party of Wm H. Seward & Co.
would, under Fremont, have
swept the whole Northern
country."    (editorial.)

[4 bottom two-thirds clipped out]

[5]
       Proem. —
Proem of all
These are the candid
     open – shown thoughts
     of me, and of all
     my body & soul
      ~~open~~
~~Lo, the amp~~ full ~~amplitude~~
        over and over
Lo the round globe, tumbling
Lo, friendly persons advancing,
        friendly
   tall, muscular, ∧ with
   sufficient hands and feet
        upon the world
Lo – ~~the~~ great women ~~of~~
       and    Lo,
  ~~the New World –~~    ~~the~~
  Now the precede  the
  beard–faced masters
 upon
  ~~of~~ the world.

[Bottom third clipped out]

[6 bottom third clipped out, blank]

[7 top third clipped out]
Lo

Shall speak in the Presidents
    Message from the porch
        Federal
   of the ∧ Capitol, and in
   the Governors' Messages
   from the State Capitols,
   and in the rulings of
   the Judges of the
   Supreme Court.

[8 top third clipped out, blank]

[9 top three-quarters clipped out]
    Commencement of Discourse

      "Spiritualism"
Life is    very    great, but there
𝑔 is something greater than life,
absorbing life, namely Death. —
When as we are in the midst
of affairs, going to dinner &c. we
receive the news of the sudden
death of —— ⁄over⟍

[10 top three-quarters clipped out, blank]

[11–12 clipped out]

[13]
        Proem
Preface of
  ∧ Endless Announcements[3487]
Toward the perfect woman
    of T̶h̶e̶s̶ America
Toward the perfect man
    of America,
Toward the President
    of These States, and
    the members of

---

3487.  Compare "Starting from Paumanok," Section 14, line 1, *Leaves of Grass,* Comprehensive Reader's Edition, p. 24: "Whoever you are, to you endless announcements."

the Congress of These
     States
     Proem
   Preface of Endless
       Announcements

    After all is said, it
remains to be said, This
too is great in its reference
to death

[14 blank]

[15]
   Poem of Remorse
I now look back to the
    times when I thought
       ?        ?
    others – slaves – the ignorant
   – so much inferior to myself
    To have so much less right

[16 blank]

[17–18 clipped out]

[19]
O you   round Earth,
    I

    Savage and strong,
    Free, luxuriant, xxx   ,
      I from Mannahatta,
      speak up for The States.

O my body, that gives
    me identity!
      all and each
O my organs !     O that
        every one
   which makes manhood!
O

                    strong
A Savage and ~~luxuriant~~
      Primal
      ~~Am~~ Free, luxuriant, *p*
           xx              I, ~~come,~~
                 ~~an Amer~~
           from Mannahatta
              stand ~~in the midst~~
                    ~~The States~~
           speak up for you and
                for These States. —

[20]
(Simply
Endless Announcements[3488]
nothing more    )
☞

[21]
Words of America
      Free and severe words,
           the master's words,

The mother's, father's,
      husband's, wife's,
      son's, daughter's words,

☞   The Proem must
have throughout
a strong saturation
of America.   The
West, the Geography,

the representative
American man.

[22]

                    g    gain
All that you do
           dissipates away

3488.  See footnote 3487.

But all that you
         do to your body,
         mind, morals, lust,
         in this sphere and
         in other spheres

[23]
Shall grow in the manly
         muscle of men and
         in the greatness of
         perfect women

---

I do not say that life
         is not beautiful,
But I say that whatever
         it is, it all tends to
         dr        the beauty of death

[5 lines of the page, clipped out]

---

                                        cements
To you, ~~endless~~ endless announ
~~T̸o̸~~ ~~You~~ whoever you are, I
         kiss you with lips of
         ~~real~~ personal
         ∧ love.

[24]
         Premonition.
(last verse
? To you, endless announcements!
? ~~T̸o̸~~ ~~America~~
Whoever
                           For your sake, these.[3489]
you are,
*     fresh and
  Free savage, ~~strong,~~
     Fluent
~~Cheerful.~~ / luxuriant,
       ~~fluent~~, self–composed –
                    persons

3489.  See footnote 3487.

[5 lines of the page clipped out]

   I was born    fond
   of the sea-beach,
In ~~the~~ streets of

          streets
~~In~~ ∧Mannahatta,        ~~I~~ walking
   ~~and so and thence~~
   I ~~sound~~
      I make
   ~~the strong~~ ∧ poems
    for
   ~~of~~  The States.
In Mannahatta's streets walking
   I make poems for The States

[25 top two-thirds clipped out]
* Free, savage, strong,
  Cheerful, luxuriant, fluent,
     composed — fond of
   self – ~~sufficient~~
   my friends, fond of women and
          children
☞▯  Fond of fish-shaped ~~Paumanok~~
   Paumanok, where I
   was born + fond of
   the sea-beach,[3490]
  From Mannahatta, I send
   the poems of The States.

[26 top two-thirds clipped out, blank]

[27]
O intertwined lands!
O lands of the future!
~~This~~
~~Ahold of hands,~~
    Copious land
    Washington's land

   3490. Compare the opening line of "Starting from Paumanok," *Leaves of Grass,* Comprehensive Reader's Edition, p. .15: "Starting from fish-shape Paumanok where I was born." Numerous other words and phrases throughout this MS were worked into the poem.

These ~~I interhanded~~
~~The interhanded States~~
  the
  O ~~my~~ lands!
~~The~~O Copious the embracing the many–armed,
   ∧ interhanded, ∧the
  knit together, the
  passionate lovers, the
   and clasped
  fused ~~ones, the equal~~
  ~~womb  offspring~~ the
  old and young brothers,
   ~~world~~ side by side
  the ~~equal~~, the
  experienced sisters
  and the inexperienced
  sisters, the equal ones,
  the womb–offspring, the
  well–~~attached, the~~
       ages! ages!
  beloved of ages! ~~and of~~
  ~~ages,~~ the inextricable,
  the river–tied and the
  mountain–tied

[28 blank]

[29 top three lines torn off]
  breezed, the Ar [ ? ]
  braced, the sea-bosomed,
  the Mississippi–drained,
  the fresh–breezed, the
  ample–land, the wonderful,
  the welcome, the inseparable
  brothers!
O dear lands! O death!
  O I will not ~~desert~~
  ~~you by death~~ be
     discharged
  ~~death be divested~~
    severed

from you by death
cannot be severed!
O I ~~do not care!~~     I
                              ~~still~~

~~will yet~~ visit you
yet
with irrepressible love.
O I ~~will visi~~ come
silently and invisibly
Again the

[30 top three lines torn off]

This then is life,
Here                    ~~arrived~~
~~This~~ is what has ~~been~~ come    upon
This ~~then is~~ the earth,
           the earth, out of
~~and what has arrived~~
~~after~~ so many throes
and convulsions. — [3491]
How curious!   How real!
Underfoot, the divine soil –
      Overhead, the sun. —
~~Afford foothold to my poems,~~
   ~~you~~
                    Earth
Nourish my poems,   and give
      them roots, ~~you earth,~~
      for they are your
      offspring,
Bedew them, ~~dews,~~ you
                         our –
      spring and summer ∧ – shelter

[31]
            Philip Holmes
         Adirondacks
— to Troy — then in the

3491.  See footnote 3485.

cars to Moreau – then
by stage to Glen's Falls –
then by stage to Lake George
– then to Scroon lake —

I will visit the Texan
     in

The ~~wal~~ jaunt over the
     Prairies as welcome as
     ever
  long ~~sail~~ voyage
The ~~banks of the~~ the
     ~~Missouri~~ up the
     ~~Mississipp~~
Shine upon them, sun, for
     they

[32]
     them, winter snows, for
     they ~~are~~ would make you
~~Help~~
Favor them, ~~to yo~~ all you
     laws of materials, and
     ~~all ponderable things~~
       of
     ~~all~~  vulgar and rejected
     things, for they would
     make you illustrious
You mothers
You  young  women,  for
      would
     they p̷ announce you
      forever
  ~~as just~~ as capable
  and eminent as
  ~~the~~ young men

[33]
   man or woman of
The ∧Texa~~n~~s, the Louisianian

the
the Floridian,    Georgian,
                    the
    the Carolinian,    Mississippian
                    the
    the Arkansian,    Californian
    as much my friend as
    ever, and I his friend
or her friend
    ∧ as much as ever,
Oregon as much mine as
        ever,
You
∧Mannahatta! ~~Mannahatta!~~
    ~~Mannahatta! still~~ close,
                            to me
        as ever! O close! close!
    man of   and woman
                of Ohio
Ø The Ohio~~ns~~        as ~~close~~ real
        to me as ever
The Kentuckian ~~my~~ for me and I for
                        him as much
        Wisconsin, Iowa,        as ever
        Michigan, Illinois,
        Indiana, Missouri.
        Kansas, Nebraska, Utah,
        Minnesota,
            as    much as
        for me    as the same    same    and I
        for them ~~as much~~ as
                    the same
        ever!

[34]
You old man and old woman,
            would show
    for they ~~know see~~    that
    you are no less
    admirable   than any

You sexual organs and
                are determined to tell
    acts, for they ~~behold~~
    you with glad
    courageous loud
    voice, to make
    you illustrious.

[35]
The Tennessee–man and
    the Tennessee–woman
        no less to me        than ever
    – the same as ever     ~~to me~~
Pennsylvania, New–Jersey,
    Delaware, Maryland,
    Virginia, yet travelled
    by me,
~~The~~ Maine, New–Hampshire,
    Vermont, Massachusetts,
    Connecticut, Rhode Island,
    New York, yet dwelt
    ~~in by me~~.
~~Huron, Erie, Mic~~
Ontario, Erie, Huron,
    Michigan, Superior,
    yet sailed upon
    by me.

[3 lines clipped out at bottom]

[36 blank, 3 lines clipped out at bottom]

[37 top third clipped out]

To you endless an
To you, these, to
    report nature, man,
        politics,    from
        an American
        point of view.

[38 top third clipped out, blank]

[39 bottom two-thirds clipped out]
These are the words of the
      master
These

[40 bottom two-thirds clipped out]
      abide
These shall live,
Shall grow in
Shall walk in the streets
      Mannahatta,
Shall climb the Alleghanies
      and

[41 bottom two-thirds clipped out]
* National hymns,
  The freeman's and freewoman's
      songs,
                  arrogant
  The master's words, ~~strong,~~
      fluent,
    ~~lawless,~~ severe. —

[42 bottom two-thirds clipped out]
      nigh   the
Dwelling ~~neighbor to the~~ Ohioan
    and Kentuckian, a
    friendly neighbor,
W Sauntering the streets of
    Boston, Portland
      long list of cities

[43 top two-thirds clipped out]
_____

  As long as the earth
    is brown and
      solid

_____

Free, savage, strong
Cheerful, luxuriant, fluent, self–sufficient

Fond of                   fond
~~Out from the sea–beach, from~~
       slender
     of Paumanok   where I was
      fond of the     sea–beach
         ~~born.~~
    From Manhattan ~~Island~~ I
       send the poems of the States.

[44 top two-thirds clipped out, blank]

[45]
Forever and
    Thy soul!
~~To cons~~

              longer
Forever and forever, ~~as long~~
     than ground is brown
   ~~as the~~
       and solid, ~~as~~ long er
  ~~as~~ than water ebbs and
flows
       their order of
in ~~a few~~
     duly ∧ millions of   years. –
They ~~gi shall~~ give place, ∧ but
    you O my soul shall never
✗  ———————— give place!

Life – how curious! how real [3492]
   and time
Space, ∧  filled with such
   easy wonders!
           delicious
To walk, to breathe, how
             the
The ~~daylig~~ day! ~~these~~
   ~~curious, o~~  ~~divine,~~
  animals,! identity,!
  eyesight!

3492.  See footnote 3485.

Underfoot, the divine
      soil,
Overhead, the sun.


[46 blank]


[47]
Listen to me,
Out from Paumanok, where
          and
    I was born, I ~~recite~~


All is in yourself,
~~The All things, all thoughts,~~
Things, thoughts, the stately
      shows of the world,
      the suns and moons,
      the landscape, summer
      and winter,   ~~the~~
      poems, endearments,
All


Free, Savage, and strong,
     ~~arrogant~~ coarse
Primal,   luxuriant, ~~coarse, and~~
         fluent
      ~~combative,~~ self–sufficient,
A   Out ~~of~~ from
 ~~O From~~ Manhattan Island
      send
    I ~~make~~ the poems
       of The States.


[48 blank]


[49]
———————      such
Fille'd fill'd with ~~wonders~~
      (the
Over–head, ~~how~~ splendid ~~the~~ sun!
Under–foot, ~~how~~ the

O divine soil!
Under–foot O divine soil!
Over, O
* How curious! – how real,
   Underfoot, the divine soil!
   Overhead, the sun!
   ~~How curious~~
   ~~How curious I myself!~~
   Me,

[50 blank]


7


1880 Notebook


[Cover:]

Whitman
      431 Stevens St:
         Camden

Dec: '80

[Inside front cover:]

[Pasted in is the front of an envelope, in William Douglas O'Connor's hand, addressed to Mr. Walt Whitman, / No. 431 Stevens Street, / Camden, / New Jersey. /, postmarked Washington, D. C., 5 May 1882.]


[1–6 clipped out]

[7–8 clipped in half, rest blank]

[9–12 blank]

[13]

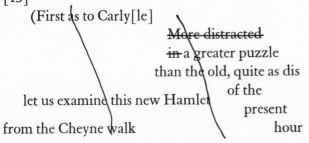

   (First as to Carly[le]
                        ~~More distracted~~
                     ~~in~~ a greater puzzle
                  than the old, quite as dis
                        of the
   let us examine this new Hamlet
                              present
from the Cheyne walk                hour

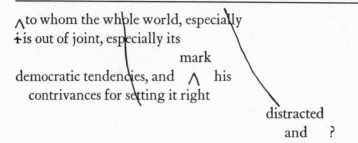

∧to whom the whole world, especially
+is out of joint, especially its
                        mark
democratic tendencies, and  ∧  his
   contrivances for setting it right

                              distracted
                         and    ?

[14–16 blank]

[17–18 clipped out]

[19–104 blank]

[105–106 clipped out]

[107–118 blank]

[119–128 clipped out]

[129–130 half clipped out]

[Notebook was turned and started over from the back to the front, but for convenience pagination has been continued]

[130 half-page remaining]
From Noon to Starry Night
Passage to India
            &
Notes as the wild Bee hums
And away from Art, away from Books
My soul and I the lesson done

[131 blank]

[132]
Songs for Good Measure


From Noon
   to Starry Night

Collections
    Clusters     namely,
& other Brochures
Passage to India
        &
    Songs
Echoes   of   62 & after
            &
Notes as the wild bee hums
Thou Mother with thy Brood
Passage to India
        &
Notes of a half-Paralytic
        or  ?
From Noon to a Starry Night
            &
Notes of a half-Paralytic

[133–146 clipped out]

[147 blank]

[148]
        Supplement Hours
        for a
Now ere I close – away from Book
Away from Art, the lesson
                    random       jotted
Sweet, Simple, costless,  ∧negligent
                                    hours
    Away                          done

[149 blank]

[150]
Nights of all Seasons
    Specimen Nights
            and the Days following
        of
Hours at Night
            made at the time

Crude Notes, intended ₓ for the
        bases of Sonnets, or a Poem
Night Affinities
            not forgetting the Days
Twilight Hours


        October Nights
        =========   also

Notes on the  &c &c
Un Pencill'd    of at the places
Momentary    Notes at the places
                    vaguely
    & times and places purposed
            as for
    vaguely for the bases of Sonnets
    or a Poem
_____

        Mrs Gilchrist
    Keats Corner   Wells Road
        Hampstead
            London
Harlakendon

[151]
    Knit Jackets
Mansfield 1417 Ridge Phil
W^m A Bryan
        3410 Haverford St
        W Phila

_____


[152]
    September Days
        & other days too
Letters of John Keats         ⎛ H B
                              ⎜   Forman
                              ⎜   editor
    to Fanny Brawne           ⎝

    Reeves & Turner
        196 Strand – pub:  London
                        Eng – 1878

Day & Night Affinities
    Last Affinities
<u>Notanda</u>    ( ?impromptu)
<u>Away</u> <u>from</u> <u>Books</u>, (after <u>writing</u> <u>one</u>)
    Impromptu Notes
        of a half-Paralytic

[Inside back cover]

  Buckle
    paper carrier
  (918 Cherry

[Pasted in are the fronts of two wrappers, of newspapers?, stamped, postmark not clear, Baltimore and Potomac Railroad printed at top, addressed to Walt Whitman, 431 Stevens St, Camden, N. J., both alike, not WW's hand]

[Back cover]

    Amherst    Canada
        Sept: '80
Knit Jackets
Kxxx    Mansfield
    1417 Ridge av

---

      Mrs  Ladd
        417 Ridge

---

[Sideways]

W$^m$ A    Bryan
3476
  Haverford
    W Phil

8

    Names — in future writing[3493]
          about the War
  for one side )  Nationals
    the        }
              } Secesh
    other   )

3493. These lines are written on a piece of paper torn from a larger sheet; on the verso is the draft of a letter to Mrs Abby H. Price, which Edwin Haviland Miller dates 1873 —see *The Correspondence of Walt Whitman*, II, 264.

## 9

### ? Names[3494]

For it is the divine genius of poets that most makes illustrious localities, and steeps them in immortal perfume, and forwards their names, like echoes of sweetest music, for centuries and tens of centuries. — This the localities of America need.

## 10

A. U. C.[3495]

Anno Urbis Conditiæ

In    the    year    the city (i. e. Rome) was built

sing          pl

arcunum — arcuna

(secrets)

"To receive a favor is to see your liberty"    Latin proverb

Habitat

residence — above

Mirabilia   latin (i. e. wonders)

L. S.   locus sigilli   (the place for the seal)

penetralia    (secret recesses)

pinxit    (he painted it)

## 11

The Oregonese are called "Webfoots"[3496]

from a letter   Salem, Oregon   Oct.   1870

[Clipping:]

### WEBFOOTS.

"And first and foremost, the people. Webfoots they are called, from a tradition that exists in California and other envious localities, that it rains here sometimes; indeed, that it rains so much that the inhabitants, on the 'natural longing theory,' receive web feet, that they may paddle around

---

3494. This title and paragraph are written on a piece of paper torn from a larger sheet.

3495. This material on Latin is written on the verso of a letterhead: George B. Carse, Proprietor. Calvin E. Linch, Business Manager. "The New Republic." No. 139 Federal Street. Camden, N.J. 187.

3496. These few words are written on a scrap of paper, to which is pasted the clipping which follows.

comfortably. I believe this to be a slander. But the people, the masses, are out in force. With a population of less than one tenth that of Wisconsin, with but one little piece of railroad of fifty miles, there are here today not less than twenty thousand people. From ten, from twenty, from a hundred and fifty miles away, men, women and children are here, in covered wagons, with tents and provisions — they come up here, some of them having been eight days in making the journey."

## 12

[1]     <u>Our Language, ~~and Future~~ & Literature</u>[3497]
       ~~Our language literature~~ and literature to come ~~the Yet too~~ much a coterie ~~The greatest~~ Of all the ~~wonderful things~~ wonder–growth's of ~~the universe,~~ humanity ~~what is more~~ nought more ~~wonderful~~ wonderful than languages/ — Of ~~all~~ languages ~~which what~~ which other is so grand, ~~and~~ has the ~~comoust~~ nature and adaptability or ~~serves~~ so well to serve us when we make it what it ~~has to~~ must be made, as ~~this~~ the English? — ~~Like Beginning form its sturdy~~ begin ~~form as we Axxx~~ Born to have [about five] an identity of its own, hundred years before the American era, — to have an identity of its own gradually strengthening and ~~tending toward flowing~~ expending to its present sturdy, and copious volume of words — ~~much~~ adopting into itself freely from ~~Celtic, Latin, Gothic, Greek, Latin Scandinavian sounds~~ [?] — many immigrancies, many clinics —

[2]     — passing through ~~many~~ changes, ~~expansions, and~~ developments — here we ~~have~~ possess it at last, ~~in These States.~~ — ~~And It is As a language not of pol~~ our most precious inheritance – greater than arts, politics, religions or greater than any wealth or any inventions.
       It is not a polished fossil language, but the true broad fluid language of ~~individuals~~ democracy. — ~~But upon it~~ Then ~~have~~ have we upon ~~it~~ it ~~we too have doubtless~~ great improvements ~~no~~ ~~Yes this language Yes~~ to make — very great ones. — ~~Large numbers of~~ It has yet to be acclimated here, and ~~fash~~ adapted still more to us and our future — many new words are ~~still~~ to be ~~added~~ formed — many of the old ones ~~made more~~

[3]     I say — The English grammarians have all failed to detect these

---

3497. This prose piece, "Our Language and Literature," heavily corrected, is written on 11 pages of various sizes and in three colors, pale yellow, yellow, and pale pink.

points where ~~our language~~ their written speech is strongest, and ~~need~~ should be most encouraged — namely in being elliptical and idiomatic, and in expressing ~~new~~ xxx ~~individual~~ new spirits. —

[4]     The English grammarians, ~~probably~~ dazzled by the ~~cold~~ lustre of the classical tongues, whose ~~genius is~~ ~~scope was~~ spirit is different from ours, ~~tongue~~ and had a different work to do, — ~~The~~ or ~~perhaps~~ likely straining to make ~~the tongue elegant~~ ~~the long rounded and granded,~~ an obedient, elegant and classically handsome ~~tongue~~ dialect, which ~~it~~ ours can never be. — (or rather the true elegance and grandeur is more ample, and lies in another direction than they suppose).

[5]     ~~A certain some smell always~~ A certain, I know not what — a kind of smell — betrays ~~all the~~ every passage of elegant writing, ~~in their Eng-lish language~~ old and new in ~~all~~ British works, that it is ~~not the~~ no fresh and hardy growth, but has been scented from outside, ~~and~~ and ~~which shortly~~ only becomes stale. — ~~Of these which follow them here~~

[6]     ~~definitely~~ to conform to our ~~genius~~ uses, — a far more complete dictionary to be written — and the grammar ~~freed from established~~ ~~for American uses, on a superior and more made into carry out~~ boldly compelled to serve the ~~g~~ ~~true~~ real ~~genius character~~ genius ~~of the language~~ underneath our speech, ~~tongue,~~ which is not what the schoolmen suppose, but wild, intractable, suggestive — perhaps in time, made a free world's language.

[7]     Indeed most of the laws of grammar, insisted on by ~~British their~~ ultramarine critics and schoolmasters, and by those who follow them here, are insisted on ~~by persons them~~ because ~~who~~ they ~~p~~ who ~~perhaps make~~ record such laws know ~~nothing at all about~~ ~~any the~~ what real grammar — ~~that which~~ is, namely the ~~grand primitive~~ law of the living structure of language in its largest sense — ~~whi and~~ often so perhaps ~~most which the spe~~ the common speech of the people ~~no lies~~ lying nearest to it. ~~This is~~ Thus ~~the~~ real grammar, vast, deep, perennial, ~~and~~ has plenty of room for ~~all~~ eccentricities and ~~all of~~ what are supposed to be ~~blunders and~~ gaucheries. — and violations. —

[8]     ~~Thus in But~~ For me, I ~~say that~~ perceive that ~~language composition~~ words ~~were~~ would be a stain, a smutchy  come deliberately ~~at~~ to the conclusion only — except for the stamina of things — ~~An is I perused~~ it have [?] it perused it — ~~Naturalness~~ Any thing ~~and its perfect~~ like the perfect beauty  sanity and beauty of nature ~~is~~ are ~~wantung in~~ is

unknown and unattempted in ~~their~~ all ~~literature,~~ the literature of England. —

[9]        ~~A great engrafting primal First~~ of The life–spirit First ~~the~~ of ~~America These~~ States must be ~~had~~ engrafted upon ~~the lan English its our~~ their ~~imported~~ inherited language: — indeed I ~~preceive~~ see the beginning of this ~~is begun~~ already and enjoy. — it. — ~~As for myself~~ I love to go away from books, and walk amidst the strong coarse talk of men ~~where there is who~~ as they give muscle and bone ~~in~~ to ~~every each~~ every word they speak. — I say The great grammar, ~~of~~ and the great Dictionary of ~~Amerie~~ the future must ~~love the same,~~ and embody it all those. — ~~It is~~ Also They are ~~almost~~ [ ? ] to follow the open voices of the Americans — for no other nation speaks with such organs as ours. ~~nation. —~~

[10]    Beyond ~~all~~ that I would like to know, indeed, Who can ~~look~~ examine these ~~best~~ type–productions of ~~English or any other foreign litera all~~ foreign ~~literature~~ literati, ~~not~~ imported here, especially ~~the English that those from~~ of not Great Britain only, ~~the rich legacy~~ of ~~almost so many hundred~~ of years but from any where, of any ages, without feeling that ~~all~~ the best, the whole, that has in them been done, ought to be ~~ought to be far be far~~ better done — ought superseded ~~here~~ here in America, ~~by things better done~~ for our own purposes?   by a newer greater ~~race of men? works? race of men?~~

[11]    ? words
        The the tendencies of other na      minds ~~are, to~~ when viewing languages, politics, religion, literature, &c ~~to~~ consider one or all of them as arbitrarily established, and ~~to~~ as ~~something~~ thus better than we are, and ~~therefore~~ thus to rule us, the ~~tendency~~ American mind shall boldly penetrate the ~~arena~~ interiors of all, ~~those things~~ and ~~con~~ treat them as servants, ~~our presses~~ only great because they ~~represent~~ forego us, and sternly to be discarded the day we are ready for superior expressions.

13

Dictionary[3498]
        Democracy
        America

3498.  This list, except for the last two lines, is written on the second page of a 54-page home-made notebook in yellow covers, sewn together; the next-to-last line is written on p. [3], and the last line on p. [12]. The rest of the notebook is blank, with a number of pages torn out, the stubs remaining.

Elias Hicks
Paumanok
Hospitals
Washington (city)
Capitol (at Washington)
West (must be before stay [?] in the heart of the west)
Mississippi
Shakespeare (with reference to America)
Alabama (aboriginal American word)
Manhattan
be put to advantage
— cruel treatment of Col. Corcoran

## 14

## Materials and Notes on Words

[Clipping from a periodical, dated May 1847, pp. 507–514, containing an unsigned review, pp. 508–513, of Joseph E. Worcester's *A Universal and Critical Dictionary of the English Language*. Whitman's notation at the top of p. 507:]

### Worcester's Dictionary

[Clipping from a periodical, dated April 1849, pp. 33–50, containing an unsigned article, pp. 34–50, "English Spelling Reform." Whitman's notation at the top of p. 33:]

### English Spelling Reform

[Clipping from a periodical, *American Phrenological Journal,* XXIV (August 1856), 26, containing an unsigned article, "The Origin of Speech, Alphabets: Their History". Whitman has underlined two passages: "The Greeks adopted the characters of the Phœnicians", and "the English alphabet will be found to consist, not of twenty-six letters only, but of more than two hundred!"]

[Clipping from the *Evening Post* (New York?), 16 or 17 July 1861, containing a two-column article, "Military Terms. Definitions of Technical Phrases".]

[Clipping from an unidentified newspaper, 1869, containing a one-column article, "How Dictionaries Are Made. The German 'Worterbuch'", taken from *The Pall Mall Gazette*.]

[Notations by Whitman on a sheet from a book:]

a good word — "rattled"   i e   confused and put out by being suddenly called on to do something

[Notations by Whitman on a sheet:]

Ex – pe – sé
Fi – ná – le
Re – su – mé
Resúme
Locale   lo-cál
Outré
Gar – rōte, (not gar-ro-te

[Notations by Whitman on the verso of a sheet containing a discarded MS article. The discarded piece reads: "13 writers of Britain are so fond of bringing against democratic institutions in general, and those of America in particular. — 'The instability of the Laws,' is not only the head and front of our offending — but the back–bone and tail — the stamina — the very nerves and life blood. — And with such instability — joined with such a newspaper literature, we are, according to the reviewer, in rapid progress upon the downward road to infamy and ruin. —

"Let us look at this matter a moment, and find if our laws are unstable — as too many even among us acknowledge  seem to suppose. — Popular opinion is fickle, we grant. — But does every change in popular opinion cause a change in the Laws, properly so called? — The mooted questions among American politicians are, items of national policy, not". This fragment is cancelled; the piece on the other side of the sheet reads:]

### Western Nicknames[3499]

The nicknames given in the West to people of different communities, are not a little amusing and sometimes characteristic. — We subjoin a list gathered by the writer, while on a steamboat journey from Chicago to Buffalo:

New–Yorkers are called Eels.

| | |
|---|---|
| Pennsylvanians — | Pennymites. |
| Missourians — | Pukes |
| Iowans ——— | Gophers |
| Ohioans — | Buckeyes |
| Michiganians — | Wolverines |
| Wisconsin people — | Badgers |

3499. See William White, "Walt Whitman, 'Western Nicknames': An Unpublished Note," *American Speech*, XXXVI (December 1961), 296–298.

Illinoisians ——— [S?] <u>Tuckers</u>
Indianians ——— <u>Hoosiers</u>
Kentuckians ——— <u>Corncrackers</u>
Virginians ——— <u>Tuckahoes</u>
Canadians ——— <u>Kanucks</u>
Oregonese — Webfoots.

15

Words[3500]

[1]    Scō ria ⎱ ashes  dross;  slag  from  a
                           smelting furnace,
   pl  Scōriæ ⎰ rejected  matter,  volcanic
                           cinders
     scorify   reduce to scoriæ
manege   place of training horses
ma nāzzh or riding – art
        of horsemanship
   malum in se ⎱ in law
   pl   mala    ⎰ a thing wrong or
                    evil in itself
mem-phí-tis  noxious exhalation
mem phi tes     especially   car-
                   bonic acid gas.
vaudevil  ⎛ variorum edition
vŏde vill ⎝ — one that contains
                 the notes of vari-
                 ous commentators
rostrum, the beak of a bird, or
                              ship
   pl  rostra    -a prominent place
                 for speaking in Ro-
                 man assemblies,
                 furnished with
                 beaks of enemy's
                 ships
personnel, the  rank  appoint-
   ments &c of persons in an
   army or other force or what-

melee
mà là
concierge  great house
                 or
kon sárj    prison
                keeper

lares
pe nā tes
manes       ghost
má nēz    shades
mememto mori  ⎛ curé (a parson
   "remember     ⎝ kú rā
       death."
mene   a Chaldaic word signifying
                       numeration
mĕ ne
mensa et thoro  "from  bed  and
                             board"
mesne  (law) middle, intervening
mēne
mezzo  méd zō (It) middle, mean
vaticinate,  to prophesy, foretell
vascular, having vessels that con-
                           tain rain
   phys          or fluids
ro–ta  (Latin) a wheel
per se  by him– her– or it self,
                          alone
         – in the abstract
Pe-ná tes – household gods
Lär, pl Lā res – ditto

3500. This long list of words, possibly for an intended dictionary, with notes and definitions, is written on both sides of five tall sheets taken from a notebook. The title, "Words," is written on the outside of the last sheet.

not, as distinct from materiel

Penchant   inclination   declivity
   pän shäng     bias

pathógnomy – the expression of
   the   passions – the   natural
   signs or science, by which
   the passions are indicated

sine qua non, "without which
                               not"

   sí ne̅     fash, (fascher, Old Fr)
                 vex, tease

en route

mauvaise honte
   mō vāź ón̂t

cón ge̅ – reverence, farewell

en famille, in a family

ang fä m̂el        manner, or do-
                               mestic

voltigeur    }  tumbler,
             }     vaulter – one
vol te zhür  }     of the light
                   cavalry

            sse

~~eclaireciment~~

eclaircissement
e klare sis m̂ang
   (the art of clearing up an
   affair. — Explanation

Pathognomy – the expression of
   the passions – the science of
   the signs by which the state
   of the passions is indicated –
   the natural language or op-
   eration of the mind, as indicated by the soft and mobile
   parts of the body.

Patois      feu de joie      bonfire
   pa twâ     fū do zhwä     gun-
                         firing for joy

comme il faut  }  as it should be
   kon e̅l fó    }

porte fuille  }  portfolio, office or de-
port fúll ye  }    partment of a min-
                   ister of state

trousseau  }  paraphrenalia, as of a
troos sō   }                    bride

feuiliage (fool ye äźh) a bunch or
                         row of leaves

eloge    a   funeral oration
ā lōzh

cuisine    kwe̅ zéne̅,  cookery,  a
                         kitchen

bass relíef, sculpture, figures not out
                   from the ground

[?]      , arrangement to attract or
                         captivate

vivace   ve̋ va che, lively
                   (musical terms)

vivacissimo         very lively

vis a vis, viz a ve̋ – face to face

surveillance  }
sur vāl yán̂z  }  inspection, oversight

Peccá vī, (Latin) "I have sinned"

Draugh or Draff (the latter pre-
                         ferred)
   refuse, swill, leavings.

Pathology – the doctrine of diseases,
   together with their causes, effects, and differences — A trea-
   tice on diseases.

[2]  Tunic  [sheet torn here]

especially Sweden and Nor-
way and Denmark)

Gaul, old France

Gaelic, relating to the Celts inhabiting the Scottish highlands, or to their
                               descendents

France

Celts, primitive inhabitants of Italy, Gaul, Spain and Britain. The[y]
    formed the first emigration from Asia into Europe 1600 B.C.
Teutonic; Teutones, ancient Germans
Saxons, the anicent inhabitants of the north of Germany
Picts, ancient inhabitants of most of the British islands, so called
    because their legs were painted

English, derived from Angles, the name of one of the Saxon tribes that passed over from Germany to England, A. D. 450

Mathematics — which treats of magnitude and number, or of whatever is capable of being numbered and measured. — Two parts—pure where geometric ma [?] or number are the subject of investiga [?] mixed where the deductions are made [?] relations which are obtained from obsera [?] and experiment.

English Language:

The Saxon speech, introduced into England, A.D. 450 is its basis or stock. On this stock, the Dane, Swede, and Norwegian ~~followed~~ engrafted much of their native speech. The Norman followed and put in the scion of the French. — Words from Latin and Greek have been freely added . . . . . . . Commerce imports words as well as wares from all parts of the earth.

Scagliola ⎱ an artificial
  skal ye ōla ⎰ marble made of
      ⎦ puverized stone

The "stroke oar": He who rows immediately by the coxwain, or foremost of rowers, pulls the stroke oar

Torso, the trunk of a statue, deprived of head and arms.

Toga, the characteristic outer garment of Roman men
Pallium, – – that of the Greeks

- repertoire  rā per toa-r

accouche! accouchez!  out with it!
    is there any gender

Préstige, illusion, imposture juggling tricks

arriere ⎱ ä    [?]
    ⎱ back, far behind,
ä ray–r ⎰ away in the in the
    rear ~~re~~

           (finish)
acheve! achevez!  out with it!

a – do – be

mo – ra – le

entree

elite

point d'appui           } a fulcrum
point d appui

Roue

[3]   touraure   [?]          [sheet torn]          or log, as of finge or jewelry

ex–e–gé–sis – the science of literary interpralate – the
author's meaning

coupon

koo poñg

façade – the front of a building

etat major     ātä–mäzhor – a specific body of officers
of the same corps

ontology – the science of being, in itself or its ultimate grounds
and conditions — metaphysics

omphalic – relating to the navel

omphacine – an oil of olives with which wrestlers
were anciently anointed

hauteur

hō toor

Bŏn–mōt   bŏng–mō – a        [?]

Bŏnne–bôuche – a delicate morsel

Bŏn–vivant    bŏn ve väñg

Bon–ton    bon tŏñ

Dieu et mon droit

deẘ a mŏ drẘä

detour

coup d'Oeil

coo dálé

(first view

slight view

hautgout

hō goo

diastole – dilation

systole – contraction

coup de main

koo de mäñg

Contour, kon tóor,
the outline or general
periphery of a figure:
the lines which bound
and terminate a figure

blancmange

blä mŏnge

a military expression
denoting an instanta-
neous

unexpected and
generally successful
attack.

da tôr – turning, winding, a circuitous way

deploy – unfold, so as to make a large front
or spread – (as a fan when opened)

debouch

debóosh, to march out of a wood or narrow
pass or file

Decámeron of Boccaccio – tales supposed to

book in

ten parts

be related during ten days

Debutant    one who makes a first appearance in public

deb ə̂ täñg

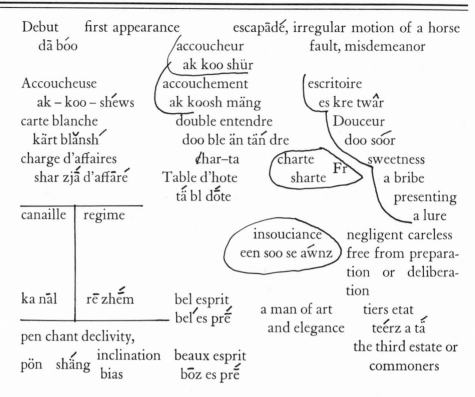

Debut    first appearance          escapāde, irregular motion of a horse
  dā bóo                    accoucheur          fault, misdemeanor
                              ak koo shür

Accoucheuse        accouchement          escritoire
  ak – koo – shĕws    ak koosh mäng        es kre twâr
carte blanche          double entendre        Douceur
  kärt blănsh          doo ble än tän dre      doo soór
charge d'affaires        ¢har-ta      charte        sweetness
  shar zjā d'affārē    Table d'hote    sharte   Fr    a bribe
                        tā bl dóte                    presenting
                                                      a lure

canaille | regime
                        insouciance    negligent careless
                        een soo se awnz  free from prepara-
                                         tion or delibera-
                                         tion
ka nāl | rē zhĕm    bel esprit
                    bel'es prē    a man of art      tiers etat
                                  and elegance      teérz a tā
pen chant declivity,                                the third estate or
  pön  shăng  inclination  beaux esprit             commoners
              bias          bōz es prē

[4]  Shäh-namah, the book of Kings, the most ancient [and] celebrated
          poem of the modern Persian language, by the poet Firdousi.
     Emerson must have been born about 1804          natal
          Bryant about 1794 or 5
     All hands, fore and aft

     All in the wind – the sail parallel in a straight line with the wind so as
         to quiver. —
     Amain, old term for yield! – now, any thing done suddenly or quick.
     Anch a–peak – anchor directly under the hawse hole
     Atrip – when the anchor hangs, perpendicularly by the cable – when the
         topsails are hoisted to the masthead to their utmost.
     Avast – stop – as "Avast heaving" stop heaving
     Back the anchor, carry a small anchor ahead large one, to help hold
     Shingle ballast-gravel. — Trim the ballast – spread it out even
     The ballast shoots – when it shifts or moves cheerily¶
     Beating to windward – sailing against the wind, by steering alternately
         close–hauled on the starboard and larboard tacks —
     Belay – make fast. — Bight of a rope, double part of a folded rope.
     Bilge – to break – The Ship is bilged – her planks are broken by violence
     Binnacle – a kind of box to contain the compasses, on deck.

Bonnet of a sail – an additional piece put on — Lace on the bonnet – fasten it on     Shake off the bonnet, take it off. —

Bow–grace – a frame of old rope or junk, put out to prevent injury from ice &c.

To break bulk, to begin to unload the ship. —

Breaming, burning off the filth from a ship's bottom

Broken-backed – as when a ship's frame is so loosened that she drops at both ends.

Capstan, by which the anchor is weighed — and other work where strong purchase is wanted.

Catheads – on the ship's bows projecting

Cat the anchor, haul it up close to the cathead

Cat's paw, a faint air of wind

Crank, too little ballast or cargo to allow much sail, or venture

Coxswain, the person who steers the boat.

Cut cable and run. — Deaden the ship's way, impede her way

Davit, a beam, used as a crane

Dead eyes; block through which the lamards off the shrouds are reeved. —

Dead lights, the shutters, at stern, used for the worst weather.

Dead water, the eddy closing around the stern as the ship sails on.

Dead wind, blowing from the very point we want to go toward

Dog–vane, a small vane, with feathers and cork, or her quarter, to show the pilot the wind.

Douse, to lower suddenly, or slacken or haul down

Dunnage, loose wood laid at the bottom ship, to keep goods from damage

Earings, small ropes used to fasten the upper corners of sails to the yards

End on, the ship advances toward the shore without any chance of stopping her.

Fake, one circle of a rope coiled

Fish the mast – apply a large piece of wood to it, to strengthen it.

[5]   To founder – to sink at sea by filling with water

To furl, to wrap or roll a sail, and fasten it to the yard

Gasket – the rope tying a sail to the yard.

The ship is girt with her cables, when too tight moored.

Ground tackle, cables, hawsers, tow-lines, warps, buoy–ropes, anchors, and every thing for anchoring or mooring.

Gybing, shifting any boom sail from one side of the mast to the other.

Halliards, the ropes by which the sails are hoisted

Hawse holes, the holes in the bows, through which the cables pass

Headway and sternway—

Heave the log over, to find the velocity of the ship —

Heave handsome, gently, leisurely – Heave hearty, strong   quick

Gib, the foremost sail, set on a boom running out on the bows

Gib–boom, a spar out of the bowsprit. — Jolly boat, a small boat.

Junk, old cable, old rope. — Jury mast, a temporary mast

Kedge, a small anchor

Keel–haul him, drag him back and forth under the keel, to punish

K I keep hold of the land, when I sail in sight of or close along the land,

Kelson, the timber over the keel, uniting to it the floor timbers

I see A good landfall, the land we wanted after a sea voyage, when first
    seen.

I see a bad landfall, the reverse

Laniards of the shrouds, small ropes at the end, to tighten them

Larboard, the left side,    larboard tack, the ship sailing with the wind
    on her left side

Lee, that point toward which the wind blows – whence the wind comes
    in windward

A fleet to leeward of another, has the lee gage

Luff! put the helm lee side of the ship, to sail nearer the wind.

Mizzenmast, the mast aft.

Neap tides, the even tides, in first and last quarter of the moon – a ship
    is beneaped when she can't float

Overgrown sea, surges rising extremely high – pay out rope.

Port, larboard. — Ratlines, the small ropes, attached to the shrouds, by
    which to go aloft

Reef, a part of the sail from one row of eyelet holes to another. — Reef
    the sail, take in one or more

Rullock; the niche in a boat's side for the oars.

Run of the ship, the aftmost part of her bottom, where extremely nar-
    row — distance sailed — also the agreement to work a single pas-
    sage from one place to another

She sands, when her head falls deep in the trough of the sea

Scud, going right before the wind — without any sail set, is spooning.

Long sea, slow long waves, uniform steady — short sea, irregular and
    broken

Settle the land, to lower in appearance, by leaning [ ? ] it away

Shank the shaft of the anchor — Sheer of a ship, her curve, from head to
    stern upon her     [ ? ]

[?]    of the anchor, a piece of wood to fit the anchor flow, and keep
it from stretching the st        [?]

[6]    Shrouds, the ranges of ropes from the mast heads to the sides of the ship,
to hold the masts.
Sinnett, a small rope, plaited from rope-yarns
Slack water, the still interval between the two tides, ebb and flow
Slatch, the period of a transitory breeze.
Slip the cable, let it run quite out, no time to weigh anchor.
To slue any thing, is to turn or veer it round – as to slue a mast or boom
is to twist it round in its cap or boom-iron.
Sounding-line, a line to sound, with marks at regular distances
To spill, to let go or discharge.
Spoon–drift, a showery sprinkle, raised by the tempest wind, and flying
before the wind. —
The masts or spars are sprung, when cracked or sprained to breaking
Spring–tides, the fullest tides at new and full moon
We stand on, we go right straight for the shore — We stand in, for
harbor
Starboard, the right hand side. — A ship is on her starboard tack when
sailing with the wind blowing on her starboard side.
Stays, large ropes, from the mast heads down before, to prevent the masts
springing [?]
Stern, a circular piece of timber, where the two sides of the ship are
united, the lower end is scarped to the keel, the bowsprit rests on
the upper end.
Stiff, the opposite of crank. ¶Wind's eye, the point whence wind blows.
Stretch out! pull    long and strong and effectually
I strike soundings, when I touch bottom with the lead.
The ship sues, when the water leaves her on shore.
Tafferel, the uppermost part of the stern.
Tamkin, the bung of wood, put in a cannon's mouth, to keep out wet.
Taunt masts, extraordinarily high masts.
tell–tale, an instrument traversing an index, to show the tiller's posi-
tion.
Tide way, that part of the river where the tide ebbs and flows strongest
Tiller, a large piece of timber, by means of which the rudder is moved.
Trunnels, long wooden pins, connecting the planks of the side and
bottom to the corresponding timbers.
Trice it up, haul it up and fasten it

Truck, a round piece of wood, tip of the flag staffs, with sheaves each
     side for the flag halyards to reeve in.
Trysail, a small sail, for cutters and brigs in blowing weather.
Unbend the sails – take them off from the yards – cast loose the anchor
     from the cable —. untie two ropes. —
To wind a ship is to ~~bring~~ change her position, and bring her head
     where her stern was.

[7]    Not graceful and free, but awkward and laborsome
       Box-hauling, veering the ship when she can't conveniently tack.
            It is done by the quickest, most expert seamanship,
       orders abrupt and decided, a cool keen eye &c
       Club hauling, a method of tacking on a lee shore.
       How shall we steer the ship, when her rudder is lost?
       Morgue    Fr (mörg)      the dead house              Gar–ro–te
            Free-liver
       Embryo, before the child is perfectly formed – after it is perfectly formed
            in the womb – Fœtus
       Ca ira Fr  sá   eŕay ("it shall go on")    French revolutionary song
       get the names of serious diseases of the eye
       Wôôld naval – to fasten or wind or intertwine a rope, as around a mast
       Díp–lō–pi a, med    a disease of the eye which causes a person to see
            double or triple
       Díp – ty – thum L, pl Diptycha. An ancient ecc. register of two leaves
            on one the living, other, the dead, saints & martyrs used in the
            liturgy
       "Kussick" "hassick" local terms used by gunners, for tussocks of tall
            grass in the bays. —
       Skălds, the musicians and poets of nearly all the northern nations. —
       — a figure – Five harps played upon by five old men with long white
            hair. ? five beautiful youths? – twenty-three full formed sinewy
            athletes. —
                                                              every man perfect
       (Play embodying character of strength savage wildness    Indian.)
            The Roman music was just as much in favor during the middle ages
       in England and France as now –
       Spirituality – Fowler's idea of the organ of "Marvellousness" which
       he calls Spirituality  is judicious. — He says it gives premonition — it
       transposes its possessor into the spiritual —

            Fore–plane, jack–plane, jointer, smoothing–plane, mallet, mortising–chisel, gimlet, augur, broadaxe

Persiflage, pár se flãzh          slobber

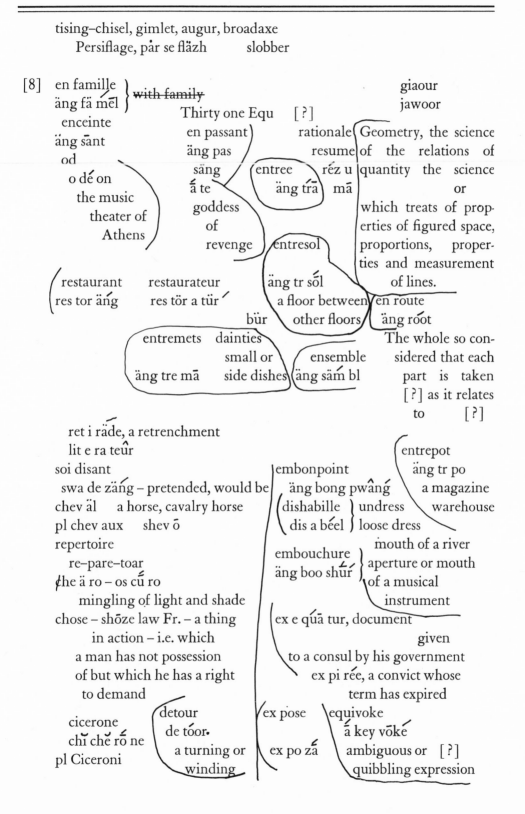

[8]  en famille }  with family                                    giaour
     äng fä mēl }                                                  jawoor
        enceinte          Thirty one Equ      [?]
     äng sãnt                en passant)        rationale  Geometry, the science
        od                  äng pas   /         resume     of the relations of
        o dé on              säng  /  (entree    réz u  quantity the science
        the music            á te      äng trá   mā              or
        theater of          goddess                      which treats of prop-
        Athens              of                            erties of figured space,
                            revenge  (entresol            proportions, proper-
                                                          ties and measurement
     (restaurant    restaurateur    äng tr sól            of lines.
     res tor äng    res tör a tür
                            bür    a floor between  en route
                                   other floors    äng róot
            entremets  dainties                    The whole so con-
                       small or   (ensemble        sidered that each
            äng tre mā  side dishes  äng säm bl    part is taken
                                                   [?] as it relates
                                                   to        [?]

        ret i räde, a retrenchment
        lit e ra teûr                                    (entrepot
     soi disant                 |embonpoint               äng tr po
       swa de zäng – pretended, would be  äng bong pwâng    a magazine
     chev äl    a horse, cavalry horse  (dishabille ) undress  warehouse
     pl chev aux    shev ō              dis a béel ) loose dress
     repertoire                                     mouth of a river
        re–pare–toar              embouchure  } aperture or mouth
     çhe ä ro – os cú ro          äng boo shúr } of a musical
        mingling of light and shade             instrument
     chose – shōze law Fr. – a thing
        in action – i.e. which  ex e qúä tur, document
        a man has not possession                given
        of but which he has a right    to a consul by his government
        to demand                      ex pi rée, a convict whose
                                       term has expired
     cicerone          (detour    (ex pose  )equivoke
     chĭ chĕ ró ne     de tóor.              á key vōké
     pl Ciceroni       a turning or  ex po zá  ambiguous or  [?]
                       winding                quibbling expression

rans des ⎱ a favorite Swiss air
vaches ⎰ of shepherds, on the
räns da väsh ⎰ Alpine horn

– ci devant    sē devăng
    formerly – heretofore
                    [ ? ]
cinque (singk) five    (in Dieu)

feuillemorte ⎱ color of
full ye mórt ⎰ a faded
                    leaf.

sans culotte
säng ku lót
boudoir ⎸ bouillon   broth
boo dwór ⎸ bool yón    or soup
bourse
boorse    an exchange

Bôu    le värd    a promenade – a
                    rampart around
                    a city

faubourg ⎰ gite a place where
jēt   one sleeps lounges
fō bóorg      or reposes on Eng
me              Ec Rev.

feme covert ⎱ a married
fāme co vért, ⎰   woman

femme sole ⎱
fām sole ⎰ single woman

fete champetre ⎸ brochure
fāte shan pātre ⎸ bro shōor
                    a pamphlet

fig-u-ránte, opera
            dancer ⎸ cabaret
bourgeois ⎱        kab a rá
boor ge wä ⎰ a citizen

[9] fiasco
[ ? ] ia
leal
prestige
maya, (illusion)
enferme (n), (an fér mé)
(confined air "the air of
    hell")
fermer (v a) (to shut up
            to coop up)
environment – environ –s
banditti (Italian)
[ ? ]        it
plus
minus
caliber
pronunciamento

peon
flume
cañon (canyon)
prairie   vaquero
            rancho
gulch
        ranchero
"my son"
"pop"    "dad"
"yes–sir–ee"
cosset
"played out"
switch off
sock it in
stay with
scantlings
slope
slide

[ ? ]  ht"
"Hymner
imperturbe (new noun)
having to do
literat, (noun meaning
        one of the literate)
        [ ? ]
bully ("bully poet")
jab – jabbed
        [ ? ]
"pawed" – ("Coburn
            pawed at
to "scull"
sluice "sluice–head"
    (in amorous) [ ? ]
shoulder–hitter
"on the shoulder"
"travels on his muscle"

a
camerilla
guachos (wắ kos
    in South America,
    Peru, Chili, &c – the
    natives, descendents of
    Europeans, mixed and
    crossed with the abori-
    gines – also more or
    less with blacks –

switch-off
dilly–dally.
take the stump
stump speech.

"muscle"
"Lorette," a modern Pari-
                sian [ ? ]
word – those of a rather
higher order, mistress,
kept woman, x[ ? ] xxx
prostitutes

Index

# Index